W9-BRY-402

The Würzburg Residence and Court Garden

Official Guide

Edited by
Werner Helmberger

with contributions by
Erich Bachmann
Jost Albert
Andreas Schumacher
Burkard von Roda
Jochen Griesbach
Damian Dombrowski

Bayerische
Schlösserverwaltung

Contents

*Putto
on
the
stove of
the White Hall
(Room 4)*

The Würzburg Residence past and present

Today the Würzburg Residence, declared a World Heritage site by UNESCO in 1981, presents above all as a place of historical interest, a masterpiece of Baroque architecture and garden design and a museum of interior design that ranks with the best in Europe. When it was built in the 18th century, however, it was primarily perceived as the representative governmental seat of a prince-bishop, in other words a clerical prince of the Holy Roman Empire, who with the proud title of 'Duke of Franconia' was also the absolutist ruler of a small state. It was from here that he governed the destiny of the Würzburg 'Hochstift', the secular territory with over 200,000 primarily Catholic subjects in 33 cities, 16 market towns and hundreds of villages, together with the even larger ecclesiastical bishopric, which comprised 300 parishes. The impressive dimensions and in particular the artistic design of the palace, which was highly modern at the time, left no visitor in any doubt of the Würzburg prince-bishop's high level of aspiration as a religious and secular ruler.

The Residence, for its day an enormous building, consisted of far more than the magnificent residential and guest rooms and the large halls for ceremonial receptions and gatherings on the main floor, most of which can still be seen today. On the ground floor in particular and the two intermediate floors, there was also an enormous number of residential and work rooms for members of the comprehensive prince-bishop court, from the father confessor to the female administrator responsible for beds. And in addition to offices such as chancelleries and registries, there were of course the indispensable service rooms such

'... it must surely be the most beautiful [palace] in Germany. The staircase is wonderful.'

Margravine Wilhelmine of Bayreuth

View of the Imperial Hall pavilion of the Residence from the east garden

5

as the linen and silver chambers, dining rooms and store rooms, kitchens and bakeries, and in the case of Würzburg of course a large wine cellar.

From the mid-13th century on, the Würzburg prince-bishops had lived for almost half a millenium on Marienberg, a hill above the town, in a building complex that had been transformed from a medieval castle into a Renaissance palace and finally into a Baroque fort. It was only after the first suites of rooms became available in the city residence built from 1720 to 1744 that they could move into an adequate governmental seat within Würzburg. But scarcely was the interior decoration of the Residence completed in 1780, when secularization and the gradual dissolution of the Holy Roman Empire of the German Nation lead to the end of the secular rule of the Würzburg bishop in 1802. After a brief period of occupation by Bavaria, Würzburg received its independence again in 1806 as a Grand Duchy before it finally became a permanent part of Bavaria in 1814. The Würzburg Residence was no longer a seat of government but merely one of the Franconian palaces belonging the Bavarian kings, who resided in Munich.

In 1918 the Free State of Bavaria replaced the monarchy and the former royal palaces were taken over by the 'Administration of the former crown estates', which later became the Palace Department. In 1921 the Residence was opened to the public as a museum, and in the ensuing decades its furnishing was rearranged in accordance with the old inventories. On 16 March 1945, one of the heaviest air raids of the Second World War almost completely destroyed the Würzburg city centre; around 5,000 people lost their lives. Most of the roofs and wooden floors of the Residence also went up in flames. Fortunately the walls and stone vaults designed by Balthasar Neumann withstood the fire, so that Giovanni Battista Tiepolo's ceiling frescoes in the Staircase and Imperial Hall were preserved.

After the initial provisional roofing and securing measures, during the postwar years the most important representative suites and the Court Chapel were reconstructed and restored. The rebuilding process was concluded in 1987 with the reconstruction of the Mirror Cabinet – although there is never an end to maintenance and restoration work with a building of this size.

Apart from the state rooms and the Court Chapel, which are the responsibility of the Bavarian Palace Administration, and the offices of the Würzburg Palace and Garden Administration, the Residence today also houses a branch gallery of the Bavarian State Painting Collections (p. 126), the Martin von Wagner Museum (p. 173) and further institutions of the University of Würzburg, the Würzburg State Archives and the wine cellar of the Würzburg State Vineyards.

View across the garden to the south façade of the Residence

Building and decoration history

By contrast with other residential palaces, the Würzburg Residence, at least externally, is not a conglomerate of various style epochs that has evolved over a number of centuries, but a new complex built from scratch according to an overall plan in only 24 years, beginning in 1720. By around 1780 the first phase of the interior decoration was also completed. One of the virtues of the Residence architecture is thus the consistency of its style, another is that here the great European architectural trends of the time, French palace architecture, Viennese imperial Baroque and the palaces of Upper Italy, are amalgamated to create a synthesis of the arts of astonishing universality. No other palace combines such a wide range of European influences as successfully as the Würzburg Residence.

Prince-Bishop Johann Philipp Franz von Schönborn (r. 1719–1724) who initiated the building of the Residence (section from the portrait in the Princes' Hall, Room 42)

FOUNDERS AND FINANCERS

The wide artistic horizons of the Residence building were primarily due to the family connections of the first prince-bishops involved in its construction. Prince-Bishop Johann Philipp Franz von Schönborn (r. 1719–1724), the initiator of the building, was from a long-established influential family, the Counts of Schönborn. Six bishops with the name of Schönborn alone ruled between the mid-17th and the mid-18th centuries, sometimes simultaneously in several ecclesiastical principalities: three times in Würzburg, twice in Mainz, Bamberg and Worms, respectively, and once in Trier, Speyer and Constance. The planning of the Würzburg building was thus a Schönborn family undertaking right from the start. Johann Philipp Franz

was advised and supported not only by his uncle Lothar Franz von Schönborn, the artistically knowledgeable Elector and Archbishop of Mainz and Prince-Bishop of Bamberg, but also by his younger brother Friedrich Carl, at the time representing their uncle as Imperial Vice Chancellor at the court of Vienna. In addition to Balthasar Neumann from Eger in Bohemia, promoted in Würzburg to court architect, who was responsible for the overall direction of this huge building until his death in 1753, the Mainz court architect Maximilian von Welsch and the imperial court architect in Vienna, Lucas von Hildebrandt, also had a major influence on the planning. The two most respected French architects, Robert de Cotte and Germain Boffrand in Paris were also consulted.

Five years after the early death of his brother, the next-but-one prince-bishop of Würzburg, Friedrich Carl von Schönborn (r. 1729–1746), was able to continue the building he already knew so well, completing the shell and also part of the interior. The next-but-one prince-bishop after him, Carl Philipp von Greiffenclau (r. 1749–1754), who was

responsible for summoning Tiepolo from Venice to Würzburg, was equally connected with the Schönborn family as Friedrich Carl's second cousin. The series of rulers involved in the building process with connections to the same family was concluded by the following prince-bishop, Adam Friedrich von Seinsheim (r. 1755–1779), who had the Court Garden laid out and the interior completed in the Early Neoclassical style – he was a nephew of the two Schönborn bishops.

The extensive network of connections and the high expectations of the rulers put the building on an almost international level not only through the architects but also through the artists and craftsmen who decorated the outstanding interior of the building, the construction of which was directed and coordinated by Balthasar Neumann. Together with them, the Residence's founders, who were involved in the details of the planning and participated knowledgeably in the decision-making, created a building that was a highlight of the German, and in fact of the European Baroque era.

From 1701 to 1704 a small palace had been built on the site of the subsequent Residence on Rennweg, but it was unsatisfactory right from the start and never occupied. This was the first attempt to transfer the court from the Marienberg fortress to the city. However, at the beginning of 1720 it was decided to pull it down on account of the rotten beams and other serious building deficiencies. This suited the purposes of the newly elected Johann Philipp Franz von Schönborn (r. 1719–1724), in that, at almost the same time, he had received the enormous sum of 640,000 guil-

Giovanni Battista Tiepolo and his son Domenico, detail from the staircase fresco

ders, which his predecessor's chamberlain, Gallus Jakob von Hohlach, had had to pay back to avoid trial for embezzlement. With this initial capital and the encouragement of the Schönborn relatives, who were equally afflicted with the Schönborn 'building bug', the plans for the new building continued to expand. The Mainz Elector and Archbishop Lothar Franz wrote to Imperial Vice-Chancellor Friedrich Carl in Vienna, telling him that the Würzburg prince-bishop, Johann Philipp Franz had found such a 'treasure' that he 'would be able to more than comfortably finance his planned residence, however expensive it might be, without adding a single penny from the treasury. So don't hold back with ideas for the building…'
This was a bit optimistic given the actual total costs of around 1.5 million guilders, but set in motion a flow of letters and visits between Würzburg, Mainz and Vienna to discuss individual variations of the plans.

The first Würzburg designs were still based on the idea of renovating and extending the crumbling little Rennweg palace with a spectacle-shaped building that had a cour d'honneur in front of the corps de logis (main wing) and two four-winged complexes on either side. However, with the encouragement of Lothar Franz, his Mainz court architect Maximilian von Welsch and other aristocratic architects associated with him, this was superseded by plans for a much larger building. One important change was the alignment of the new building's central axis with the top of the bastion forming part of the Baroque city fortifications that lay behind the Residence to the east. In this

Balthasar Neumann, detail from the staircase fresco

way the triangular slope leading up to this bastion could be transformed into a garden symmetrically aligned with the building, albeit one that would be most unusual for the Baroque age. On its north side the new building could only go as far as the Rosenbachhof and the Rennweg, the road that ran in front of it to the city gate, and the central axis that the planners had chosen limited the possibilities of widening the palace on the south side. Additional space could only be gained by increasing the building's depth. Quite soon, therefore, a 169-m-wide ground plan with three wings emerged, and the two side wings that each took up around a third of the width were then considerably expanded to form the sides of two inner courtyards lying one behind the other. The initially rather hesitant Prince-Bishop Johann Philipp Franz, whose priority in those precarious times was the extension of the city fortifications, was persuaded by Lothar Franz

13

to agree to the gigantic project, because after completion 'few or almost no other residences in the whole of Germany will rival it for appearance, commodiousness, layout, symmetry and everything a princely residence should have'.

Large palace buildings are almost all joint creative achievements. And in the case of the Würzburg Residence, quite apart from the constant involvement of the prince-bishops and aristocratic architects, neither Balthasar Neumann nor any of the other architects had the sole authority over the project. The planning process was thus fittingly described as 'collectivist'. Neumann had only arrived from Eger in Bohemia in 1711 as a 24-year-old with a training in gun and bell foundry, and had begun studying geometry, land surveying and civil and military architecture in Würzburg, supported by loans from his home town. Two years later he joined the Würzburg military, took part as an engineer in the siege of Belgrade under Prince Eugen in 1717 and subsequently also visited the imperial city of Vienna and Milan. In 1718, after his return to Würzburg, he was appointed a captain of the engineers. Neumann had little experience of civil architecture, so that in 1720 he was only at the beginning of his career as one of Germany's greatest Baroque architects. However, he took advantage of the unique opportunity to participate actively in the planning of the Residence right from the start as one of the few building experts on the spot. Although his task involved juggling the proposals and plans of Maximilian von Welsch and Lucas von Hildebrandt with the wishes of the ruler, with growing experience he was also able to produce increasingly appropriate solutions of his own. All the Schönborns recognized Balthasar Neumann's great gift, including the Würzburg prince-bishop who entrusted him with the direction of the project – initially together with the experienced Bamberg court architect Johann Dientzenhofer.

educated man of the world with considerable political influence as Imperial Vice-Chancellor in Vienna. Balthasar Neumann now had to deal not with the Mainz or Paris architects but to an increasing extent with Lucas von Hildebrandt, whose work the new prince-bishop considered to be 'the best architecture of the day'. Hildebrandt was a difficult and extremely irascible character, but Neumann nevertheless assured the prince-bishop that he would 'probably get on' with him. In 1730 Neumann went to Vienna with new proposals, in 1731 Hildebrandt came to Würzburg. Neither the prince-bishop nor his architects wanted to implement the outdated Mainz or Paris ideas as they were. A plan drawn up by Neumann in 1730 represented an attempt to replace the typically Baroque ovals of Maximilian von Welsch with rectangular projections. Otherwise the façades of the cour d'honneur and the garden front were already the main focus of attention, with the considerable involvement of Hildebrandt, even though the central building was to be constructed last. In 1730 the south block was begun with its cour d'honneur and city wing. The shell of the Court Chapel was built in 1732–1733, after Neumann had succeeded in relocating it to the southwest corner of the south block. By the end of 1733, the four-winged sections on both sides had been roofed, with the exception of the ovals. In 1734 there was a temporary hold-up in the work due to the War of the Polish Succession. However, since the whole middle section had no basement, the back walls of the cour d'honneur and the south garden façade were already going up in 1735. In 1737 the staircase was begun. The cour d'honneur façade of the corps de logis was finished in 1738, except for the ornamental pediment, and the roof of the White Hall was completed, followed in 1739 by the roofs of the Staircase Hall and the Imperial Hall. In 1740 the garden front was also complete up to the north pavilion and in 1741 the entire shell with the exception of the Northern Oval was

Court Garden gate, wrought-iron work by Georg and Anton Oegg, 1748–1774

roofed. In 1742 the large vaulted ceilings in the Imperial Hall and the White Hall were built, followed in 1743 by the Staircase Hall ceiling. The wrought-iron work for the cour d'honneur designed by Lucas von Hildebrandt was constructed in 1739–1744. In December 1744, 24 years after the laying of the foundation stone, the shell was finished and a celebration of thanksgiving was held with 16 Masses. One year later, in 1745, both Maximilian von Welsch and Lucas von Hildebrandt died, followed in 1746 by Friedrich Carl von Schönborn, one of the main influencers of the building project.

As the north block was built first, the rooms in the city wing of this section were already being decorated under Prince-Bishop Christoph Franz von Hutten (r. 1724–1729) as the First Episcopal Apartment, even though they were never completed (cf. Rooms 30–39). Important fragments of the stucco-work by Johann Peter and Karl Anton Castelli have been preserved from this first interior, which was designed by Germain Boffrand in the Régence style; they were incorporated into the subsequent redecoration of the suite of rooms in the Neoclassical style.

However, the interior decoration only achieved an international standard under Friedrich Carl von Schönborn (r. 1729–1746). Although the Second Episcopal Apartment in the cour d'honneur and the city wing of the south block that was furnished for him in 1735–1737 was replaced at the beginning of the 19th century by the Tuscany Rooms (today the art gallery of the Martin von Wagner Museum), much of the Baroque and Rococo decoration completed during his reign, from 1735 in the Court Chapel and from 1740 in the Imperial Apartments, has been preserved. The design of the interior was no longer influenced by Paris, but by the imperial capital of Vienna, especially during the first phase of decoration that ended in 1738 with the death of the court painter and designer Rudolf Byss, who had come to Würzburg via Prague, Vienna and Bamberg. In Würzburg a wide range of influences were incorporated through the work of gifted artists and craftsmen from a variety of origins. The individual artists included the stucco-worker Antonio Bossi from Porto Ceresio on Lake Lugano – the 'ornament genius' of the Würzburg Residence – the versatile sculptors and carvers Johann Wolfgang van der Auwera from Würzburg and Georg Adam Guthmann from near Schweinfurt, the gifted cabinet-maker and woodcarver Ferdinand Hund from

Upper Swabia, the brilliant court locksmith and wrought-iron artist Johann Georg Oegg from Tyrol, who like the court potter and porcelain maker Dominikus Eder had come to Würzburg from Vienna, and the Byss pupils Anton Joseph Högler, Johann Thalhofer and Georg Anton Urlaub. The constant interchange of artistic ideas in this international group of artists produced an independent Rococo form of remarkable individuality – 'Würzburg Rococo', one of the richest and most exuberant of all the variations of this style in Germany. This brief but exquisite flowering of Franconian art produced some of the finest interiors in Germany and beyond.

With the decoration of the Imperial Apartments, the two particularly luxurious state and guest apartments on either side of the Imperial Hall, the Würzburg Residence continued an older tradition of German palace building, which had spread during the Counter-Reformation, especially in Catholic parts of Germany. In theory, the two apartments consisting of Antechamber, Audience Room, Bedroom and other rooms were designed as appropriate accommodation for the imperial couple, in case of a visit. In Würzburg such visits were actually to be expected, because of the proximity to the election and coronation locations of Frankfurt and Mainz. Franz Stephan von Lothringen, on his way to his election as emperor in Frankfurt, stayed from 2 to 4 July 1745 in the Second Episcopal Apartment. His wife Maria Theresia stayed here somewhat later on 20 September 1745, when she spent the night in the Southern Imperial Apartments on her way to join him for the coronation. Over the years the Imperial Apartments were used in practice as guest rooms for other high-ranking guests and as state rooms for receptions.

After the death of Friedrich Carl von Schönborn, the fate of the still unfinished Residence rooms at first hung in the balance. His successor, Prince-Bishop Anselm Franz von Ingelheim (r. 1746–1749), who was only interested in alchemy

and making gold, dismissed Balthasar Neumann and stopped the building work. This unhappy interlude, however, ended only three years later with Ingelheim's death.

The following prince-bishop, Carl Philipp von Greiffenclau (r. 1749–1754), a second cousin of the Schönborn bishops, immediately reinstated Balthasar Neumann as building director. Under Greiffenclau a further high point

The continent of Africa (section) from the ceiling fresco above the staircase by G. B. Tiepolo, 1753

of the interior was achieved with the engagement of the greatest fresco painter of the 18th century, Giovanni Battista Tiepolo, who arrived from Venice at the end of 1750. Apparently Greiffenclau was not entirely satisfied with the ceiling painting in the Garden Hall that had been completed shortly beforehand by Johann Zick from Lachen near Memmingen. By July 1752 Giovanni Battista Tiepolo,

The cour d'honneur gates, which were pulled down in 1821, on an engraving from 1757.
Detail from the illustration on p. 10/11

engaged on generous terms, had painted first the three frescoes in the Imperial Hall, which featured the wedding of Emperor Friedrich I Barbarossa and Beatrix of Burgundy in 1156 in Würzburg and the investiture of the Würzburg bishop by this emperor in 1165–1168. In 1752–1753 Tiepolo then created the largest ceiling painting that had ever been produced for the huge dome vault in the Staircase Hall, showing the sun rising above the world with allegories of the four continents, the glorification of the prince-bishop as a patron of the arts and portraits of some of the artists involved with the Residence. Rooms of such dimensions and dynamic conception were a challenge, even for Tiepolo, who was at the zenith of his creative powers. Here two great works of European architecture and painting combine to form spectacular syntheses of the arts. At the end of 1753, shortly after the death of Balthasar Neumann, Tiepolo left Würzburg after an almost three-year stay. A year later Prince-Bishop Carl Philipp von Greiffenclau also died. The era of Würzburg Rococo had come to an end.

COMPLETION, DESTRUCTION AND RECONSTRUCTION

It was during the reign of Prince-Bishop of Würzburg and Bamberg Adam Friedrich von Seinsheim (r. 1755–1779), a nephew of the Schönborn bishops, that the transition from the Late Rococo style to Early Neoclassicism began. Between 1763 and 1772 the stucco-workers Friedrich Manger and Ludovico and Materno Bossi, nephews of Antonio who had since died, worked through the Northern Imperial Apartments from the Bedroom to the Green Lacquered Room. The still uncompleted walls of the Staircase Hall were decorated in 1765–1766 by Ludovico Bossi with stucco-work in the 'goût grec style', a form of Early Neoclassicism, while Franz Anton Ermeltraut added Neoclassical grisaille painting to the Vestibule. In 1772 the Princes' Hall, designed at Seinsheim's request as a princes' gallery, was decorated with stucco-work by Materno Bossi. The rooms of the First Episcopal Apartment, the so-called Ingelheim Rooms that were designated as an additional guest apartment, were completely redesigned in the Neoclassical style and also decorated with stucco-work by Materno Bossi in 1776–1778. The garden-lover Seinsheim also had the Court Garden laid out and the square in front of the Residence acquired its final form from designs by Neumann's pupil Johann Philipp Geigel in 1765–1774. Balthasar Neumann had already conceived the huge square as a magnificent stage, on which the many aspects of this huge building would appear, as it were, in various acts, both in sequence and in unison. An important part was played here by the cour d'honneur gates, designed by Lucas von Hildebrandt and completed in 1744, which closed off the courtyard and swung out into the square outside. Georg Oegg had made the wrought-iron grilles, Johann Wolfgang van der Auwera the stone figures and obelisks on the pillars and sentry boxes, including two over 3.40-m high Hercules groups. To balance the Rosenbachhof on the north side of the square, Johann Philipp Geigel built the Ambassadorial Building on the south side with a replica façade and added arcades on both sides, each terminating in high columns. The work was completed in 1774.

With the advent of secularization in 1802, the episcopal principality of Würzburg was abolished and its territory fell first to the Electorate of Bavaria. From 1806–1814, however, it regained its independence for a few years as a new Grand Duchy under the government of Grand Duke Ferdinand III of Tuscany. Ferdinand, who came to Würzburg as a widower with young children, had three large apartments redesigned in exquisite Empire forms by the Frenchman Alexandre Salins de Montfort for the use of a future wife and his daughters. These Tuscany Rooms took up three wings on the main floor of the south block and the cour d'honneur wing of the north block. With the end of the Napoleonic era, Ferdinand III returned to Florence and Würzburg finally became part of the new kingdom of Bavaria under King Max I Joseph. His son, Crown Prince and future King Ludwig I, frequently resided for longer periods with his family in what was now the Royal Palace of Würzburg. In this way the Wittelsbachs sought to forge a closer link between the population of the new Franconian territory and the Bavarian monarchy. On 12 March 1821, the youngest son of Ludwig and future Prince Regent Luitpold was born in one of the Tuscany Rooms of the Residence. In the same year the magnificent cour d'honneur gates, together with the sculptures and sentry boxes, were regrettably pulled down. As a result of this barely comprehensible decision (even though it had been considered since 1783), a central element of the original finely balanced structure and design of the square is missing. The replacement planned by Leo von Klenze for Crown Prince Ludwig consisting of stones linked by chains and again two sentry boxes was never built.

From the end of monarchy and the foundation of the Free State of Bavaria in 1918, the former royal palaces were administered by the Bavarian Palace Administration. From 1921 the Residence was open to the public as a museum, the buildings and gardens were restored in line with conservation principles and the interior was furnished in accordance with the old inventories.

On 16 March 1945 disaster struck Würzburg and the Residence. A heavy air raid set the whole city ablaze and with it the roofs, wooden ceilings and floors of the Residence. Only the outer shell and the rooms with stone vaulted ceilings, which fortunately included Balthasar Neumann's magnificent suite of rooms in the corps de logis with Tiepolo's frescoes, withstood the inferno. This was largely due to the excellent vault construction technique of Balthasar Neumann, who, against the advice of Lucas von Hildebrandt, risked spanning the immense spaces in the Vestibule, Staircase Hall and Imperial Hall with unsupported stone ceilings. In 1945 his vaulting also withstood the burning debris but was then exposed to the elements. In the following months, Tiepolo's frescoes would have been irreparably damaged by damp, if it had not been for the commendable action of the American officer of the

Monuments and Fine Arts Section, John D. Skilton, who promptly obtained the necessary wood and felt for the provisional roofing. Further securing and repair work was carried out by the Bavarian Palace Administration, and by 1950 the Staircase Hall and corps de logis had largely been restored. The last topping out ceremony took place in 1959, but for structural reasons, further complex measures soon became necessary to ensure the safety of the building: in 1964–1966 the corps de logis was provided with a supporting steel casing and the double columns between the Vestibule and Staircase Hall were replaced by massive pillars.

Meanwhile, since a new use had to be found for large sections of the Residence, various state institutions were now housed here (Würzburg University, the Martin von Wagner Museum, the State Archives and the offices of the State Vineyards, etc.). At the same time, the work of restoration continued systematically and without interruption. One of the greatest achievements was the restoration of the Court Chapel, which was reopened to the public in May 1963. The reconstruction of the Tuscany Hall in the university section was completed in 1965. The difficult, laborious restoration and partial reconstruction of the state apartments was also commenced. This was possible because the movable furnishings had been removed and stored during the war, and large sections of the wall panels had also survived the fire. The Southern Imperial Apartments (with the exception of the Mirror Cabinet) were completed in May 1970: This was followed in 1972–1974 by the Northern Imperial Apartments, and in 1974 the State Gallery was also reopened. The Ingelheim Rooms and the Princes' Hall have been accessible since 1978. In 1981, the Würzburg Residence, including the square in front of it (Residenzplatz) and the Court Garden, was included in UNESCO's list of 'World Cultural and Natural Heritage' sites and placed under special protection. Reconstruction

of the Mirror Cabinet in the Southern Imperial Apartments was completed in October 1987. More extensive restoration operations were carried out room by room, beginning with the Staircase Hall in 2003–2006 . This was followed by the Imperial Hall in 2006–2009, the Court Chapel in 2009–2012 and the Garden Hall in 2014–2106. In three exhibition halls open to the public since 2014, items of furniture are once again on display from the Tuscany Rooms destroyed in the war (Room 13a–c) and in 2015 a Memorial Room was created to document the war damage of 1945 and the measures undertaken to save the Residence by the American officer of the Monuments and Fine Arts Section John D. Skilton (Room 11).

The war-damaged Residence with the first new roofs, as it looked in 1947

Court Garden

Although the history of the Court Garden is as old as that of the Residence itself, it was only in the reign of Prince-Bishop Adam Friedrich von Seinsheim (r. 1755–1779), when the palace was basically complete both outside and inside, that the project progressed beyond the stage of preliminary planning. All the plans were conditioned by the architecture of the palace and the available terrain. The main limitation was the fact that this was not a summer residence but a city palace that was still within the walls, though on the periphery of the city. As the possibility of making a breach in these walls was never seriously considered, the space available for the usual palace gardens was limited right from the start. There was only room to the east and south of the Residence. And as the Residence is a complex of many different types of palace architecture, so the Court Garden is not symmetrical and uniform in style but consists rather of several sectors of virtually independent design which spread out in different directions from the south and east fronts of the Residence and are combined into a loose artistic unit only by the architecture of the palace itself. The total area of the gardens, however, is little more than three times that of the Residence. A classical French layout with canals and avenues stretching away to the horizon was, therefore, out of the question from the beginning. Building and garden not only had to respect the existing bastions, they had to make them part of the composition. The Residence is in fact located at the base of the symmetrical but stilted triangle formed by the bastion, so that its main architectural axis coincides with the apex of the triangle and is directed to-

View of the flowerbeds framing the south garden

wards the tip of the bastion. It was thus not the architecture of the palace but the bastion that was the determining factor! The extended main axis of the Residence is capped by the bastion, so that the space is dominated by the architectonic energy of the bastion, not of the Residence. The layout of the garden had even less in common with the French style in that the terrain between the Residence and the bastion, at least in the later plans, was not flat and even, but rose in three terraces to the height of the rampart, from which a waterfall was designed to cascade. It was not the extended architectural axis of the Residence but the splendid amphitheatre provided by the bastion that determined the layout of the east garden section. This more intimate portion of the garden was clearly influenced by Italian rather than French traditions, as well as earlier forms of German garden design going right back to Furttenbach.

The situation was rather different in the garden in front of the southern lateral façade of the Residence. The layout of this section was determined by the Residence alone and not by the existence of a bastion. The parterre extends from the southern lateral side façade of the palace front and is bordered on the opposite side by the orangery. It consists of a rectangle subdivided in the style of Austrian gardens by paths running along the main axes and diagonals, with a circular basin in the centre. Here however, the main axis, which is an extension of the oval projection of the façade, is noticeably the least developed, the path being not only narrower than all the others but also obscured by two groups of statuary. The main emphasis is on the path that cuts across the rectangle, dividing it into two unequal halves and thereby bending the diagonals and diminishing their effect. This path runs parallel to the south façade, meeting the avenue running from north to south, which is the real main axis of the whole garden complex: it functions, as it were, as the hinge between the two sec-

tions of the garden, each of which opens out in a different
direction, the first one to the east, the second one to the
west. It was not the axis leading from front to back, as in
French garden design, but rather the transverse axis, as in
many German gardens, that was important here. Between
these two areas, there is a garden in front of the south-east
edge of the Residence that serves to link the two main
sections and was thus usually designed as a maze or hedge
garden. Adjoining this feature was the open-air theatre
that was almost obligatory in the gardens of Germany.

This concept of the garden, which in many respects was
governed by the architecture of the Residence and the na-

ture of the terrain, was maintained from the 1720s through all four stages of development until its final implementation in the 1770s. Only details were altered, most of which improved on the original plan.

In the earliest plans dating from 1722–1723, the east garden appears either as a level space with six basins or already as a terraced garden with a cascade; all the plans however provided for an orangery as the termination of the extended main axis. At this stage the design of the south garden was strictly symmetrical, with four formal beds surrounding a central basin. The south-east section linking the two main gardens was to have a gallery of lime trees and already an open-air theatre. Maximilian von Welsch's designs show richly structured but somewhat schematically arranged formal flower beds. The extended main axis in front of the imperial pavilion is not however emphasized by paths but sensibly obscured through the division of the garden into small sections.

An interesting innovation in garden planning, which went far beyond the concepts current in Italian and French garden design at the time, was introduced by Balthasar Neumann's plan of 1730, which for the first time incorporated the summit of the rampart in the layout. On top of the rampart, which he made accessible with a system of terraces, ramps and steps, he planned a promenade along the boundary between the gardens and the open countryside. This promenade was to encircle the two bastions in front of the south and east gardens and provide a view, as from a balcony, over the gardens on the one side and the countryside on the other. A central feature of the English landscape garden, the encircling path or belt, thus makes its appearance here in an otherwise strictly geometrical concept at a surprisingly early date, although by no means for the first time on the Continent (cf. the Hermitage at Bayreuth).

In a series of plans developed in 1738, Balthasar Neumann replaced the schematic, Austrian-style articulation

of the south garden by a parterre with a very sophisticated structure and abundant formal beds, and introduced lateral sections rather like hinges to relate it as a whole to the east garden. The court gardener Johann Demeter finally laid out the south garden in 1756–1758 according to the plans of the architect and captain Johann Michael Fischer, a pupil of Balthasar Neumann. In addition, in 1759 the Bavarian court architect François Cuvilliés the Elder, and in 1767 also Balthasar Neumann's son, worked on the design of the grand flight of steps. The Seven Years' War however held up the work to such an extent that on Demeter's death in 1769 the south garden was still unfinished

View of the east garden with the steps, ramps and terrace walls on either side

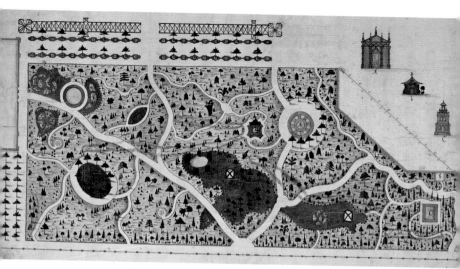

Geigel's design for the landscape garden section in the southwest part of the Court Garden

and the east garden not even begun. Real progress only began when Adam Friedrich von Seinsheim summoned Johann Prokop Mayer, a native of Bohemia, to Würzburg in 1770 and appointed him court gardener. Mayer, who had learnt his craft in France and had recently been employed in England, showed remarkable appreciation of the situation, and designed for the Würzburg Residence ('one of the most beautiful palaces in Europe') not an English landscape garden but a symmetrical geometric complex which surpassed everything hitherto planned or completed, while in no way abandoning the original concept. On a similar principle to Balthasar Neumann's suites of rooms, he conceived a series of 'garden rooms' which abutted or interlocked to form a complex whole. In front of the Imperial Pavilion was a circular sunken parterre with fountains, which extended into the second terrace and was laid out with radial and bell-shaped sections and formal beds. Ramps and peripheral pergolas led up to the second terrace, where there was a small, intimate cabinet garden

(Princes' Garden) with a basin and cascade. Flights of steps on either side of the garden led from here up onto the ramparts. Mayer employed all the devices of centuries of garden tradition, and with its spatial contrasts and intersections, this small but sophisticated complex of gardens was unique in Germany in its day.

By contrast with the terraced east garden, the south garden formed a rectangular 'garden hall'. It was extended to the west by a hedge garden and a further axis was also added, angled towards the tip of the second bastion. The exceptional Neoclassical garden statues, mostly of Savoyard boys, putti, vases and cartouches, were created by Johann Peter Wagner and his atelier from 1771 as well as the two groups 'The abduction of Europa' and 'The abduction of Proserpina' on the central axis of the south garden, which date from 1777. (During the 20th century the stone sculptures were gradually replaced by sculptor's copies or casts). This section is bordered on the south side by an orangery built in 1756–1758.

The Rococo wrought-iron gates at the entrance from the court promenade with the small coat of arms of Prince-Bishop Anselm Franz von Ingelheim on each gate wing, completed by the court locksmith Georg Oegg in 1748–1751, are a generation older. In 1764–1766 Oegg then added the side grilles, which were additionally crowned with the monogram of Prince-Bishop Adam Friedrich von Seinsheim in Late Rococo forms.

When the latter died in 1779, the gardens were still not quite finished. In the meantime garden design had progressed far beyond the creations of Johann Prokop Mayer. The Würzburg Court Garden was now outdated, as the English landscape garden had revolutionized garden design throughout Europe. Prince-Bishop Franz Ludwig von Erthal (r. 1779–1795), who like his brother Friedrich Carl, the Elector and Archbishop of Mainz, was an adherent of the English landscape garden, rejected the old geometri-

Section from
a plan of the
Würzburg Court
Garden dating
from 1803.
To the right of
the two oran-
gery wings are
the grounds of
the St Afra
Monastery,
surrounded by
a wall

cal style of the Court Garden as 'affected and contrived'. The cascade planned for the east garden was thus never built and the area south of the Residenzplatz was converted in 1793 by bailiff Geigel into a landscape garden. For a long time during the 19th century the garden was maintained more as a museum piece, but in the last few decades a moderate renovation programme based on conservation principles has been implemented. This has included clearing away the trees and shrubs that had grown in profusion around the magnificent amphitheatre in the east garden, obscuring its elaborate structure.

THE KITCHEN GARDEN SOUTH OF THE ORANGERY

In the 17th and 18th centuries, numerous court kitchen gardens were designed on ornamental principles and displayed with pride as gardens in their own right. At the beginning of the 19th century, a representative kitchen garden was also laid out in the Court Garden of the Würzburg Residence. It was located south of the orangery and occupied an area of approximately 5,000 m² which had been separated off shortly beforehand from the neighbouring monastery of St Afra and surrounded by a wall. The outstanding features of this kitchen garden at the edge of the Court Garden were the artistically clipped fruit trees and espaliers. The original design with an almost right-angled grid of paths and ten vegetable beds of similar size remained almost unchanged until the 1960s. The central and transverse paths were lined with tall fruit trees, pruned to form alternating conical and open funnel shapes. These elaborate forms have been almost entirely forgotten, but were widespread in gardens at the end of the 18th century. The fruit that ripened on the crowns of these trees was of excellent quality and was served to the court as dessert fruit. In the course of the 20th century, the

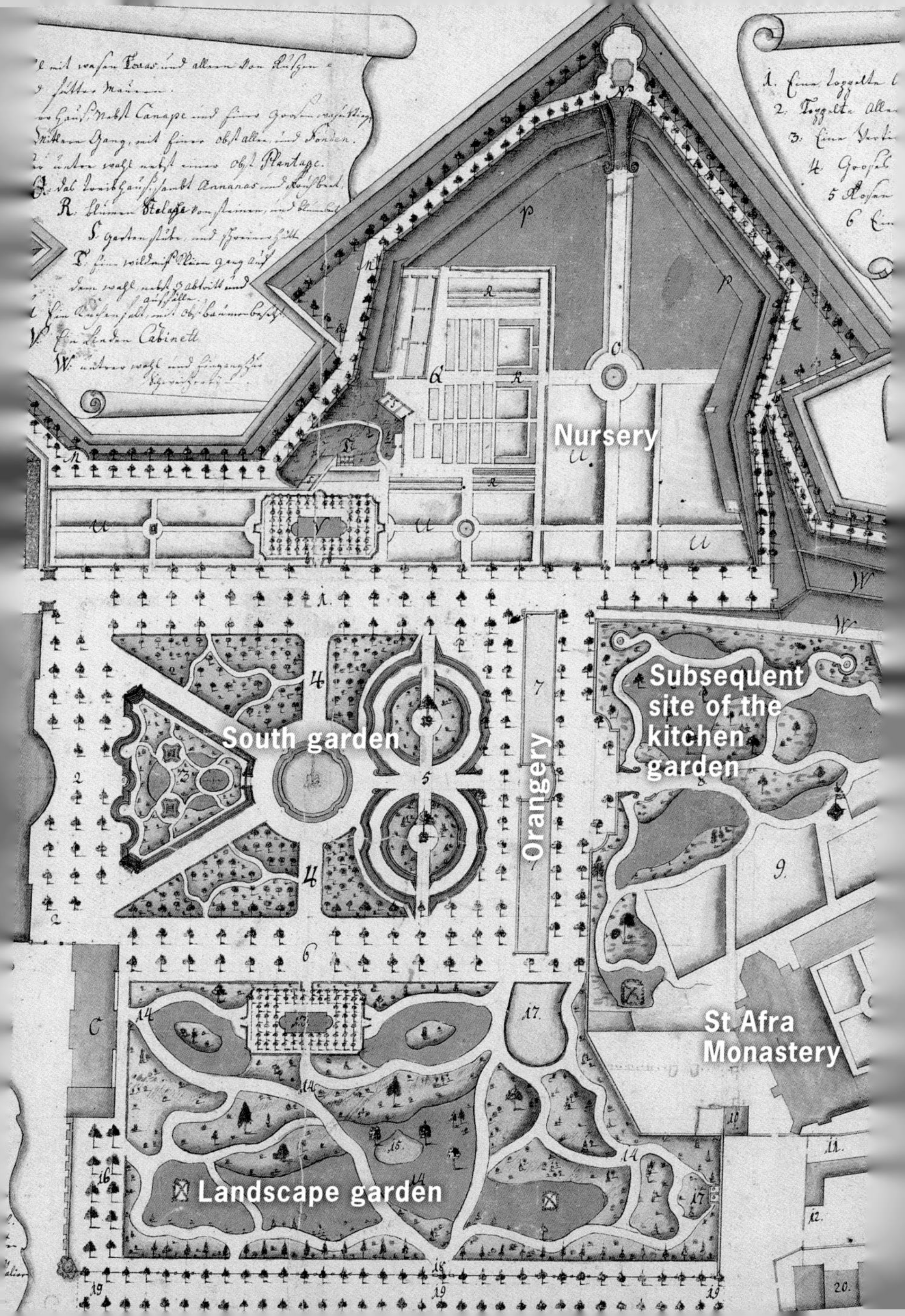

Nursery

South garden

Subsequent site of the kitchen garden

Orangery

St Afra Monastery

Landscape garden

The orangery with the kitchen garden in front of it

Right: Section from the original cadastral plan with the south part of the Court Garden, 1837

cultivation of useful plants gradually became less important and finally ceased in 1969. After the fruit trees had been felled and the old vegetable beds levelled, they were replaced by a simple lawn with a path around it and a row of linden trees along the wall of the neighbouring Kilianeum. In front of the terrace wall of the orangery and the western enclosing wall there was a bed with perennials and shrubs and a few seats. In 1997 the Bavarian Palace Administration decided to recreate the kitchen garden with its original structure of beds and paths and to plant it with historical and new varieties of fruit and vegetables. The reconstruction of the kitchen garden took place in three stages from October 1998 to September 2001. Over 120 tall fruit trees and just under 60 berry-bearing shrubs were planted. In the next few years the crowns of the fruit trees will be shaped as they were at the beginning of the 19th century, so that future visitors to the Würzburg Court Garden will once again be able to admire the horticultural art of fruit-tree clipping.

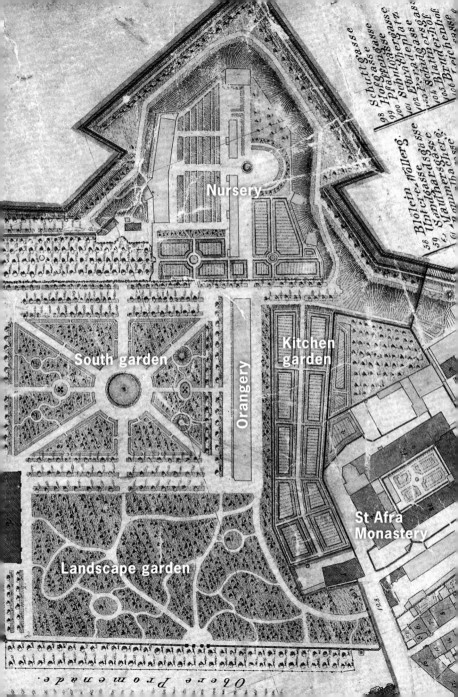

Nursery

South garden

Orangery

Kitchen garden

Landscape garden

St Afra Monastery

Blotein Möllerg.
56 Unteresse
59 Sandgardsgasse
54 Maulhergasse
Baumergner.
Baumerhasse

Obere Promenade

Residence Square and the façades on the west front

The spacious Residence Square (Residenzplatz), now sadly used as a car park, formed a stage on which the massive bulk of the Residence was separated off from the old part of the city and presented as an architectural event that could be viewed from many angles. The existing features were skilfully incorporated into the design: the Rosenbachhof built before the Residence in around 1700 from a design by Joseph Greissing (on the pediment the Rosenbach-Stadion marriage coat of arms) was adapted as the left-hand wing building and in 1767 the Ambassadorial Building was added as a counterpart with the same façade by the court architect, Johann Philipp Geigel. He then also designed the arcades and high columns that gave the 190-m-wide square an additional depth of 115 m, extending it as far as the filled-in moat of the medieval city wall. The fine wrought-iron grilles in the arcades were created by Georg Oegg, and the Neolassical sculptures (replaced with copies) are the work of Johann Peter Wagner. As the visitor crosses the square, which slopes upwards slightly towards the centre, it is the façades of the two massive side blocks, the so-called twin palaces that first attract attention. It is not until the centre of the square is approached and the visitor enters the cour d'honneur – which was originally separated from the square by the gates built across it in 1739–1744 (demolished in 1821) – that the massive building opens up in a U-shape to form a more intimate space leading to the pompous main façade of the central building.

The façade system, which was already established when the north block was begun, has four storeys, with two mezza-

'... no palace in the whole of Germany can compare with this one.'

Lothar Franz von Schönborn

The central projection in the cour d'honneur behind the Franconia Fountain by Ferdinand v. Miller, 1894

nine floors above the much higher ground and main floors. However, because of the banded rustication the two lower storeys look like a single bottom floor, which extends as far as a continuous cornice and has the effect of raising the main storey. Above the upper mezzanine is a console frieze supporting an attic balustrade decorated with sculptures. The height of the building up to the upper edge of the balustrade is around 22 m. The city fronts of both side blocks each have two three-axis projections, with pilasters on two of the floors and triangular pediments. In the middle of each of the seven axes between these projections is the driveway into the courtyard, emphasized by half columns on either side that support a balcony. Above the wrought-iron archway grille (made by Johann Michael Lintz in 1728 on the north side, and by Georg Oegg on the south side) is an escutcheon between pairs of putti bearing the initials of King Max I Joseph of Bavaria, which was added in the early 19th century. Above the balcony is a door window between double pilasters, with a round arch decorated with trophies and supported by two herm atlantes. The remaining main floor windows are roofed with pediments or arches with cartouches that were originally filled with the coats of arms of Würzburg canons (removed in 1803). The cartouches of the north block are crowned solely by the prince's hat, and it was only the wings built later on by Friedrich Carl von Schönborn that also featured the imperial crown, which this prince who was also Bishop of Bamberg was entitled to include in his coat of arms. The triangular gables of the side projections have reliefs (now copies) by Jacob van der Auwera, the father of Johann Wolfgang, with allegories of justice and the common good (north block) and of harmony and piety (south block). Beneath the latter, on the ground floor is the portal leading to the Court Chapel, which introduces an element of asymmetry and tension into the façade. The trophies on the roof balustrade are the work of Claude Curé.

The four inner courtyards have a simpler façade structure, which is limited to frames round the windows and cornices separating the floors. The entrances in the courtyards have projecting panels with pilasters. The transverse wing between the courtyards of the north block still has the frames for high round-arched windows from the earlier plans for the chapel. The corresponding transverse wing in the south block has a ridge turret with the court chapel bells.

The cour d'honneur façades of the side blocks are all structured with pilasters. They also consist of seven axes between two three-axis projections, which in this case projects by a whole window axis. While the projections no longer have pediments, they each have four columns in front of the façade that support a frieze and above this a wide balcony. Here the projecting frieze only covers the windows of the lower mezzanine, but in the axes between the projections it replaces them and there remain only three floors. Instead the ground floor here has high arched windows; originally these 'seven arches' were even planned as open arcades with balustrades and they were only closed off with windows as building progressed. In the central axis is an entrance framed by half columns with a small balcony above it.

The emblems and ornamentation are at their most elaborate on the nine-axis main façade of the cour d'honneur with three-quarter columns across the entire width. The three-axis central projection with the three large entries into the Vestibule is a massive, six-column portico. The three high arched windows on the main floor, which belong to the White Hall, extend to the upper mezzanine. On the roof balustrade, which is more elaborately decorated here, are figures of gods and busts of emperors (copies). The reduction to only two floors in the central pavilion is undoubtedly due to French influence. The front appears more monumental as a result – measured by human proportions – but compared with all the other façades it looks

lower. The building complex dips in the middle, despite the enormous, elaborately designed pediment above the central projection. This large show pediment is a characteristic feature of Lucas von Hildebrandt's work: two lions hold the coat of arms of Prince-Bishop Friedrich Carl von Schönborn, crowned with the prince's hat, and above this with the imperial crown.

The overall impression of the façades is dominated by the slate roofs: the attic roofs of the corner pavilions and the curving roof behind the central projection. The façades, built of greenish-yellow sandstone, did not originally show the stonework, but were painted 'in a natural stone colour': the structural elements were silver grey against an ochre background, and the sculptures on the attic and the cour d'honneur gates were white, with gilded attributes.

Two wrought-iron gateways like triumphal arches flank the city front of the Residence: to the left the Rennweg

Gate, and to the right the gate by the Ambassadorial Building. In the ornamentation on top of the Rennweg gate, which was made from 1751 by the court locksmith Georg Oegg, the side section has the initials of Prince Bishop Carl Philipp von Greiffenclau (r. 1749–1754), while the middle section, which was not completed until 1767, bears the initials of his successor Adam Friedrich von Seinsheim (r. 1755–1779). Since Seinsheim was again also Prince-Bishop of Bamberg, his coat of arms culminates in the imperial crown (this entrance never had actual gates and the lower side grilles, which were taken out for pedestrian traffic, are on display in the Bavarian National Museum in Munich as examples of Franconian wrought-iron work). The side grilles of the gateway by the Ambassadorial Building leading to the Court Garden were already made by Georg Oegg in 1748–1749 and show the coat of arms of Prince-Bishop Anselm Franz von

The west façade of the Residence has a total width of 168 m

Ingelheim (r. 1746–1749). The middle section made in 1769 by Georg's son and successor Anton Oegg was only added in 1774. The crowning ornamentation is still in the Rococo style and is a somewhat smaller copy of the one on the Rennweg Gate, while the gate wings were purely Neoclassical.

The trefoil-shaped Franconia Fountain in front of the cour d'honneur was planned on the occasion of Prince Regent Luitpold of Bavaria's 70th birthday (r. 1886–1912) as a 'memorial expressing the love of all the Franconian people'. Three years later, on 3 June 1894, the prince regent ceremoniously unveiled the fountain. The bronze figures – the allegory of Franconia with the Franconian artists Walther von der Vogelweide, Mathias Grünewald and Tilman Riemenschneider sitting at her feet – were made in the Munich foundry of the younger Ferdinand von Miller.

SIDE FAÇADES AND GARDEN FRONT

The side façades of the Residence, 92.7 m wide, have the same four-storey structure across all 21 window axes as the wings on the city side. The only distinguishing features of the three-axis projections on either side are the pilaster structure and the attic roofs. The most striking features are the five-axis half ovals projecting from the centre, which were Maximilian von Welsch's idea and are emphasized by double pilasters and impressive roof caps. The 169-m-wide garden front also has four floors throughout, except in the central pavilion. At either end are shallow projections, each with five axes and a three-axis column portico supporting a balcony. On the main floor the segmentally arched window pediments are crowned with trophy sculpture. The triangular pediment above is decorated with allegories of peace and war in relief. The high point of the garden front – and here the influence of the Viennese architect Lucas von Hildebrandt is most evident – is the five-axis central pavilion, a projection forming three sides of an octagon, which contains the Garden Hall and Imperial Hall. It has a further floor above the eaves and the most elaborate sculptural decoration. On the ground floor the high window arches of the Garden Hall extend into the first mezzanine, and pillars support the large balcony in front of the Imperial Hall. The high arched windows of this hall have half columns on either side; the window pediments on a level with the upper mezzanine are decorated with trophies, vases and putti. The attic floor with the clerestory windows of the Imperial Hall is structured with the herm pilasters typical of Hildebrandt's style. Above this is the curved pediment that was originally decorated with lions holding the coat of arms of Friedrich Carl von Schönborn. This was replaced in the early 19th century by the initials of King Max I Joseph of Bavaria. The eleven axes of the four-storey façades between the end projections have segmentally arched window pediments filled with ornamental decoration. To achieve the transition to the central pavilion, the two axes on either side of it are separated off by double pilasters and more elaborately decorated. Most of the sculpture was made by Johann Wolfgang van der Auwera, with the additional involvement of Claude Curé and other sculptors working on the Residence. From a distance, this façade is also dominated by the attic roofs of the pavilions, in particular the curved roof of the Imperial Hall pavilion.

On the far right of the garden front the north garden gate (Greiffenclau Gate) closes off the Court Garden from the Rennweg. The wrought-iron grilles of this gate were created in an exuberant Rococo style by Georg Oegg 1751–1752. In the middle centre piece is a large reproduction of the coat of arms of Prince-Bishop Carl Philipp von Greiffen-clau (r. 1749–1754), the head beneath is a self portrait of the wrought-iron artist.

Halls in the central block

1 VESTIBULE

View of the staircase from the Vestibule (prior to the reinforcement of the double columns in 1964/65)

The Vestibule was made extraordinarily wide in order to accommodate the three large entrances insisted on by the building's founder, Johann Philipp Franz von Schönborn. The vaulting, executed with remarkable technical skill, could not be made any higher because of the White Hall above, and is alarmingly shallow. The unsupported hall is so spacious that even coaches drawn by several horses could enter and turn in it. On either side, four massive pillars separate off a passage three steps up and also mark the beginning of the Staircase Hall. The central transverse axis was originally only flanked by double columns, but these had to be replaced in 1964–1965 for structural reasons by more stable pillars. Only the twelve atlantes, sculpted out of the rough stone by Johann Wolfgang van der Auwera in 1749, remain from the first phase of decoration. The Neoclassical stuccowork was created by Ludovico Bossi in 1765–1766, and the illusionistic grisaille painting in the ceiling panel, with a view into a dome with the labours of Hercules, by the painter Franz Anton Ermeltraut. The two marble statues in the niches of the south wall, Minerva and Bellona, are the work of Johann Peter Wagner and date from 1779. The entrances originally had fanlight grilles inserted by Georg Oegg in 1749–1750; after 1821 the door wings were redesigned by Leo von Klenze.

2 GARDEN HALL (SALA TERRENA)

The Garden Hall projects from the garden front with three sides of its octagonal ground plan, and was originally intend-

Garden Hall with ceiling fresco by Johann Zick, 1750

ed to have wrought-iron gates leading into the garden instead of windows. Because of the Imperial Hall above it, it is no higher than the Vestibule. The graceful, light impression it makes in spite of this derives from the brilliant structure designed by Balthasar Neumann. Twelve columns standing away from the walls, arranged in a rectangle but not occupying the corners, support an oval central vault that is surrounded by an ambulatory with vaulted rectangular bays and triangular spandrels. On the walls opposite the columns, multicoloured marble monoliths, are pilasters made of stucco marble. Striking use is made of colour with the yellowish-white, red- and blue-tinged marble columns and stucco pilasters with contrasting capitals. The vaulting rises effortlessly from them like the jet of a fountain and as a result the central vault stands out from the walls like a baldachin.

The charming stucco decoration created by Antonio Bossi in 1749, has light-blue motifs on a white background, pierced

Diana in repose, detail from the ceiling fresco by Johann Zick in the Garden Hall

by sparkling fragments of mirror. The ceiling painting was produced by Johann Zick from Lachen near Memmingen in 1750. It opens the low vault to give a view of heaven, but the dark, earth-brown tones introduce an element of heaviness into the room. The picture shows a 'Banquet of the gods with the banishment of Saturn from Mount Olympus' and 'Diana at rest'. It has now been discovered (Büttner 2008), why the sinister cyclops with an eye in the middle of his forehead sitting at the table as a guest of the gods. It was with weapons obtained from the cyclopes that Jupiter had succeeded in driving his father Saturn from Mount Olympus. The ousted Saturn (on the right with wings and scythe) fled across the sea to Latium, which had a golden age under his kingship. In the vaults of the ambulatory, twelve putti scenes represent the four elements, the seasons and the times of day. The two life-size stucco sculptures on pedestals, each consisting of three figures, are late, previously unidentified works by Antonio Bossi dating from 1761.

Staircase Hall, view from the landing

Architecture and painting combine to make the Staircase Hall at Würzburg one of the most magnificent interiors ever achieved in a secular building. Originally, at the wish of the building's founder, there were to have been two relatively small staircases in the conventional horseshoe shape, one on each side of the Vestibule. The plans were then extended to provide for three flights of stairs with landings, similar to the staircase finally constructed. Balthasar Neumann wrote home from his Paris trip in 1723 to say that Germain Boffrand was of the opinion that there should only be one 'main staircase on the left-hand side' 'with a large gallery round it', which had also been one of Robert de Cotte's suggestions. Neumann finally enlarged the remaining staircase into a monumental five-bay complex that extended as far as the north courtyard. In addition, he eliminated the supporting cornice from the upper storey and the surrounding vault and achieved a brilliant technical feat by spanning the whole space measuring 19.0 x 32.6 m with a single unsupported dome vault. Construction began in 1737, the room was roofed in 1738 and by 1743 the vault was finished. According to a story told by Balthasar Neumann's son about his father's rival, Lucas von Hildebrandt, the great Viennese architect declared that he would 'have himself hanged at his own expense' under the vault if it should hold, whereupon Balthasar Neumann countered by offering to have a battery of artillery fired off under it. At any event the vault held and even withstood the disastrous air-raid in March 1945.

Originally the walls of the stairwell were not solid around the first landing but opened up by arcades to the ambulatory on the ground floor. The staircase itself is set like a light-filled framework with three bays into a vast five-bay hall; the complicated, lively display of rising and falling flights and counter-flights, terraced landings and connect-

ing galleries changes constantly and looks different from every stair. The effect would have been further enhanced with the elegant balustrade by Georg Oegg or the stone parapet by Ferdinand Tietz with fragmented rocaille work that were originally envisioned as alternatives. However, neither of these ideas were put into practice, and ten years after completion of the vault Tiepolo found the room still without its final balustrades and wall stucco-work.

It was probably Giovanni Battista Tiepolo who came up with the bold idea of filling the massive vault with a single continuous painting that began immediately above the main cornice rather than dividing it up into several small fresco fields. With the fresco he painted in 1752–1753, the largest one ever produced, he created the perfect decoration for Balthasar Neumann's architecture. It is not known whether Tiepolo was given a specific picture programme, as he was for the Imperial Hall. The general topic can be identified as 'The sun rising above the world', embodied by the sun god Apollo and the allegories of the four continents. The most important iconographical idea, which is however incorporated on a modest scale into the overall composition in the form of a portrait medallion, is the glorification of Prince-Bishop Carl Philipp von Greiffenclau (r. 1749–1754) as a patron of the arts and the sun of Franconia.

Tiepolo's basic idea for the composition, which was both simple and effective, was to put the continent allegories with their numerous figures into a frieze above the main cornice, with one continent per side, above which there is an expansive view of a cloud-filled heaven peopled by ancient gods. The huge painting cannot be seen as a whole from any one position, but is deliberately angled towards various points in the

Two sculptures on the stair balustrade: Spring...

room and reveals itself gradually to a person climbing the stairs. From the landing at the top of the lower centre flight of stairs, all that can be seen is the short northern side with the allegory of America and the northern half of the heavens. At the top of the picture is Apollo, who appears before the gloriole of the rising sun to begin the day's journey, with his chariot below and his steeds being led from the clouds to the right. To his left beneath him on the banks of cloud, which are piled up to a great height, are the four seasons represented by gods with Mars and Venus below them on the dark cloud in front of the quadrant with the signs of the zodiac representing the months.

The dark cloud above the America scene casts a shadow over its right-hand half, also darkening the two stucco-work giants which frame the corner field. America is presented as a majestic female figure with a crown of feathers and a bow, who is riding on a colossal alligator. A page is offering her hot chocolate, and she is pointing to a banner, on which is possibly the griffin from the Greiffenclau coat of arms. America is portrayed as a continent rich in game, fruits and other natural resources, but still uncivilized, which is how it was seen in the Baroque age. The decapitated heads beneath the alligator's jaws and the campfire scene on the right, towards which a European with pointed shoes is creeping, might even be a reference to cannibalism.

As the visitor starts to climb the counter-flight, the short south side of the fresco comes into view. The main topic of the composition here, above the allegory of Europe, is the glorification of Carl Philipp von Greiffenklau, whose portrait as a picture within a picture is being borne aloft by the genii of fame and virtue into the heavenly realm of the gods. The prince-bishop's ermine-lined cloak spreads out behind the oval por-

... and Winter, by J. P. Wagner, 1771–1776

59

trait, which is crowned with the prince's hat and has a griffin, Greiffenclau's heraldic animal, clinging to the lower edge of the picture frame. On the banks of clouds behind are Jupiter with Ganymede, Saturn, Vulcan and Diana; hovering above them is Mercury, who is gesturing towards the sun god Apollo in the other half of the picture. The allegory of the European continent is understandably full of references to the Würzburg court, which represents the whole of Europe as a superior civilization and treasury of the arts. Even the architectural backdrop on the left features the Northern Oval of the Residence, while the scaffolding round the structures next to it might be a general reference to the building enthusiasm of the prince-bishops. On a throne directly beneath the prince's crimson cloak is the allegory of Europe, with her right hand bearing the sceptre resting on the horns of a bull garlanded with roses. The globe at her feet characterizes Europe as the queen of the whole world, while the allegory of painting to the left of this, who is staring up with a surprised expression at the portrait of Greiffenclau just snatched from beneath her brush, and the musicians to the right of the throne identify her as a patron of the arts. The pages bearing a crozier, episcopal cross and mitre represent the bishopric of Würzburg, but also Europe as the centre of the Christian religion. Beneath the musicians a dog sniffs at the architect Balthasar Neumann, accurately portrayed, who is reclining on the cornice. As a colonel of the Franconian artillery, he is seated on a cannon, but is depicted wearing the uniform of a heyduck. Here Neumann is representing architecture as a whole, while the man in the brownish-white cloak with the attributes of a sculptor, who is possibly Antonio Bossi, represents sculpture. By including real portraits, which today can no longer all be identified, Tiepolo enriched what was actually an impersonal and timeless allegory with interesting contemporary documentation. The page in a blue doublet on the left behind the allegory of painting is almost certainly Lorenzo, the younger son of Giovanni Battista, and the lieutenant with the horse next to him may be Ignaz Michael Neumann, the 20-year-old son of the architect. Giovanni Battista Tiepolo's own portrait with a red-brown cap and a white scarf is located between the two stucco giants in the left-hand corner. Next to him are perhaps his two closest colleagues, on the right his elder son Domenico as a gentleman with a powdered wig and on the left the Viennese painter and gilder Franz Ignaz Roth who worked in the Residence for decades.

The allegories of the continents of Africa and Asia, in much longer friezes above the two long sides of the room, are only completely visible from the opposite gallery on the upper floor. Above the east wall is the princess 'Africa', enthroned on a dromedary. A kneeling Moor with a sunshade swings a censer, and in the foreground are elephant tusks, cloth and a vase. The river god Nile, accompanied by a pelican, serves as a topographical reference. In the centre above the medallion of a Caesar, an African offers European dealers jewellery, to his left are further merchants and porters with bales of goods, casks, etc. Africa is depicted in general as a continent with abundant treasures and flourishing trade relationships. In the foreground Tiepolo painted an anecdotal scene: a monkey has evidently just been thrown off an ostrich which is hastening away.

The allegory of Asia on the west (cour d'honneur) side is dominated by the figure of Asia, enthroned on an elephant, who like Africa opposite is gesturing towards the portrait medallion of the prince-bishop and hence emphasizing his worldwide fame. Asia is surrounded by flag-waving soldiers, subjects on their knees and prisoners naked on the ground, begging for mercy. On the left a big cat is slinking towards a group of men in front of a wooden hut while on the right is Calvary with crosses and pilgrims, with the toppled statue of Diana of Ephesus at

Next double page: Balthasar Neumann and other artists at the court of Europe, section from the ceiling fresco above the staircase by G. B. Tiepolo, 1753

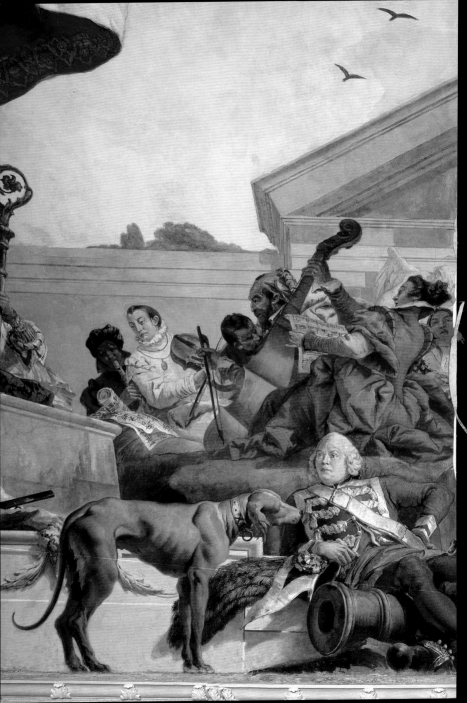

the foot; on the far right is a group of people by an obelisk. On the cornice is a large block of stone with the Armenian alphabet and next to it a smaller one bearing the signature of the artist: BATTA TIEPOLO F. 1753. The continent of Asia is presented here as a developed but warlike civilization, and at the same time as the place of origin of the Christian religion and the writings that had also produced the first works of architecture and sculpture.

With the masterpiece he completed in 1753, Tiepolo made the effect of Neumann's Staircase Hall even more overwhelming. The ascension from the dimly-lit forest of columns on the ground floor into the radiant brightness and hall-like spaciousness of the unsupported upper floor was now combined with the gradual revelation of teeming exotic worlds and a vertiginous view of an apparently endless heavenly realm of the gods.

It was not until 1764–1765, a decade after Tiepolo's departure, that Ludovico Bossi was commissioned to decorate the walls of the upper floor, with the requirement that they

must be in the latest style, 'à la grecque', a precursor of Neoclassicism. He took over the arrangement of pilasters that was probably designed by Neumann, gave them Neoclassical stucco bases and capitals and also created an elaborate profile for the entablature in the style of the time. On the two long walls he filled in the mezzanine windows and used the resulting space for tropy decoration and putti at play, with interesting painted shadows. On the south wall adjoining the White Hall are four busts as allegories of the seasons, surrounded by putti, and on the north wall four medallions with heads in the ancient style. In the central axes are Fama and Chronos, with cartouches that are now empty, but were probably intended for the coat of arms and initials of Prince-Bishop Adam Friedrich von Seinsheim (r. 1755–1779). The originally open arches in the walls of the stair well were closed by 1771–1772 and in 1774 Materno Bossi, a brother of Ludovico, supplied a massive chandelier made of gilded stucco-work (destroyed in 1945).

The continent of Asia, from the ceiling fresco above the staircase by G. B. Tiepolo, 1753

On the balustrades, which were made from 1767, are allegorical and mythological figures created by Johann Peter Wagner in 1771–1776: along the central flight of stairs are the four seasons, on the east flight Apollo and Paris representing music, on the west flight Meleager and Atalanta representing hunting. Some of the figures on the balustrade of the upper floor have plinths that are not the right size for the particular location, indicating changes of plan or rearrangements. The individually very attractive allegories have still not been convincingly interpreted. It was not until 1776, when Wagner produced the final sculptures that are already masterpieces of another age, that the Staircase Hall was actually completed, 33 years after the vault was built and 23 years after the fresco was finished.

4 WHITE HALL

As part of the suite of large halls in the central block, the White Hall has several functions. It was deliberately designed with muted colouring to heighten the effect of the colours in the following Imperial Hall. Functioning as a central link in the sequence of rooms, it provides access from the Staircase Hall on the north side to the Imperial Hall on the east side and also to the Second Episcopal Apartment on the south side. And from its windows on the west side there is a view of the cour d'honneur and the Hofstrasse newly created by Balthasar Neumann to provide a vista of the cathedral with its adjacent Schönborn Chapel. The decoration of this hall in 1744–1745 under Prince-Bishop Friedrich Carl von Schönborn is perhaps the most impressive work of the brilliant ornamentation artist Antonio Bossi. Under pressure due to the expected visit of the prince-bishop, he and his assistants filled the room in only four months with spectactularly inventive, new forms of stucco ornamentation in white on a grey ground. It was a singular achievement on the part of An-

tonio Bossi to cover the immense wall spaces of this hall as well the astonishingly high vaulted ceiling with such an intricate form of decoration as the rocaille. His extraordinarily three-dimensional rocailles are full of life and movement, rippling over the vault and cascading into the room.

The hall was originally intended as a 'salle des gardes', (guard hall) as can be seen from the war trophies and the figures of Mars and Bellona, as well as the emblems of the episcopal principality incorporated into the stucco-work. Of the three doors leading into the Imperial Hall, the two outer ones were only added in 1752, hence the stucco-work griffins with the escarbuncles from the coat of arms of Prince-Bishop Carl Philipp von Greiffenclau (r. 1749–1754) that appear above them. On the north wall is the original grey marble fireplace with the Schönborn coat of arms; its counterpart opposite was replaced in 1769 with the Neoclassical stove made by Anton Oegg from a model by the court cabinet-maker Franz Benedikt Schlecht. The sculptures decorating the stove, an eagle and four putti representing the seasons made of terracotta and covered in beaten metal, are the work of Materno Bossi, who was also responsible for the stucco-work of the new niche.

Paintings: Portraits of Prince-Bishop Friedrich Carl von Schönborn (r. 1729–1746; 2 portraits) and Prince-Bishop Anselm Franz von Ingelheim (r. 1746–1749), all three German c. 1740/50, as well as a portrait of Prince-Bishop Adam Friedrich von Seinsheim (r. 1754–1779) by Franz Lippold, 1755–1756.

Furnishings: 2 console tables with the Schönborn coat of arms and 2 others, all carved and stained dark brown, Würzburg, c. 1745 (workshop of Georg Adam Guthmann) ▪ 2 vases, Japan, 18th century ▪ 2 alabaster vases, Italy, c. 1710 ▪ 57 sconces with metal foliage (49 three-armed, 8 five-armed) with a gold varnish, Würzburg, c. 1770 ▪ 5 crystal chandeliers, Vienna, c. 1750.

▣ IMPERIAL HALL

The Würzburg Imperial Hall – this name was already used in 1754 – is one of the last in a long series of similarly designated halls, and from an artistic point of view probably the most important of all. Imperial halls are a typical feature of many Baroque residences of electors and ecclesiastical rulers in the Catholic regions of Germany. Rooms of this kind began to appear in the Counter-Reformation at the beginning of the 17th century, and usually feature series of portraits of emperors and the glorification of the idea of empire or wise and beneficial government. The Imperial Hall in Würzburg thus does not explicitly pay homage to the ruling imperial House of Habsburg, but with the depiction of two events that even then dated back

around 600 years, refers to the independently ruled bishopric or Duchy of Würzburg's long-standing status as part of the Empire and the mutual benefits resulting from this relationship of trust.

The vaulted ceiling of the Imperial Hall was already finished in 1742, but the room was only decorated and furnished under Prince-Bishop Carl Philipp von Greiffenclau (r. 1749–1754). The decoration of this unique work of interior art is the work of three equally gifted artists: the architect Balthasar Neumann, the stucco-worker Antonio Bossi and the fresco painter Giovanni Battista Tiepolo.

When entered from the White Hall, the ground plan of the Imperial Hall presents as a transverse octagon measuring 25.90 m by 16.40 m. 20 three-quarter stucco-marble columns with gilded composite capitals along the walls support the entablature halfway up which runs round the entire room. Above this, forming a transition from the octagonal to the oval, is a stilted dome vault with a flattened vertex

71

at a height of 15.70 m. Three sides of the hall with large arched windows correspond to the central pavilion projecting from the east façade. On the slanting inner walls are marble fireplaces beneath mirrors and bishop portraits, and on the long inner wall are the connecting doors to the White Hall, some of them with mirrors. In the short sides of the room are the doors to the Imperial Apartments as well as two arched niches with life-sized stucco-work statues of gods by Antonio Bossi: Neptune, Juno, Flora and Apollo who represent the four elements. Projecting from the middle of the entablature on the long sides are the gilded stucco coats of arms of Friedrich Carl von Schönborn and Carl Philipp Greiffenclau by Franz Lippold, who also painted the fireplace portraits.

The vault is dominated by ten large lunette caps that extend far up into it, and ten large lunettes, three of them blind windows. Between the lunettes on each of the slanting sides, a continuous trapezoid vault panel runs from side to side across the narrow ends of the hall. This provided space for two further frescoes in addition to the one covering the flattened vault vertex. Four large Viennese crystal chandeliers bathed the hall in a festive light.

In 1735 the Würzburg Jesuit fathers Seyfried and Gilbert, probably commissioned by Friedrich Carl von Schönborn, had already designed a picture programme for the halls of the Residence that consisted of numerous historically important topics. As one of five (!) scenes, the Staircase Hall was then going to feature 'the wedding of Emperor Friedrich and the Burgundian princess Beatrice and the confirmation of the Würzburg bishop Herold's privileges and his investiture with the Duchy of Franconia'. The events from the 12th century that are summarized here were taken up under Prince-Bishop Carl Philipp von Greiffenclau and became the general topic of the three frescoes in the Imperial Hall, described in detailed written proposals.

The wedding of Emperor Friedrich I Barbarossa and Beatrix of Burgundy, fresco by G. B. Tiepolo in the Imperial Hall, 1751–1752

Next double page: Emperor Friedrich I Barbarossa granting the Würzburg bishop Herold the Duchy of Franconia at the Imperial Diet of Würzburg in 1168, fresco by G. B. Tiepolo in the Imperial Hall, 1751–1752

O. BTTA. TIEPOLO 1782

Via Würzburg merchants working in Venice, Prince-Bishop Greiffenclau succeeded in engaging the already famous Giovanni Battista Tiepolo, for whom it was the first fresco commission outside Upper Italy. On 12 December 1750 the painter arrived in Würzburg with his two sons, the 23-year-old Giovanni Domenico and the 14-year-old Lorenzo, and began drafting the work. It was reported on 27 April 1751 that 'Painter Diepolo began tracing and painting the pictures in the main hall today'. One year later, Tiepolo was already signing the third fresco in the Imperial Hall and on 30 June 1752 he received the follow-up contract for the Staircase Hall.

The fresco above the short southern wall depicts the wedding of Emperor Friedrich I Barbarossa and Beatrix of Burgundy. Heavy stucco curtains, pulled aside as on a stage, reveal the interior of a large church, where the bridal couple is kneeling to receive the blessing of the bishop. This politically significant wedding took place in Würzburg in 1156. The marriage gave Friedrich the important Free County of Burgundy and brought Burgundy back into the Empire. Tiepolo vividly illustrates the host of wedding guests: the Chancellor of the Holy Roman Empire with drawn sword who stands beneath the banner with the imperial eagle, a page bearing the imperial crown, two court ladies, several princes of the Holy Roman Empire, on the far right the Marshal of Franconia with the ducal sword and in the foreground a court dwarf kneeling on the steps. Neither the church nor the costumes are from the 12th century, however. The slit puffed sleeves and knee breeches, oversized collars and neck ruffs from the 16th century had to suffice in the 18th century for a credible depiction of a historical event.

On the short northern wall opposite, two events that happened at different times are combined in a single scene: Emperor Friedrich I Barbarossa grants the Würzburg bishop Herold the Duchy of Franconia and confirms his ducal privileges. The first event took place in 1165, probably

during a court assembly, and the second in 1168 during an Imperial Diet, both in Würzburg. In the picture the then bishop Herold, bearing the ducal flag, kneels before Barbarossa and swears the oath of allegiance. Tiepolo updated the political statement of the picture by giving the historical Würzburg bishop the features of the current office-bearer Greiffenclau for whom he was working. Instead of setting this scene as the programme required in the 'Princes' Hall, where the estates of the Holy Roman Empire are gathered', Tiepolo placed it in a Mediterranean landscape. Barbarossa is seated on a marble throne between statues of Hercules and Minerva. On the right is again the Chancellor of the Holy Roman Empire, as an old man of gigantic build bearing a drawn sword on his shoulder. On the left are pages bearing the bishop's cope and the ducal hat. In front of the triumphal arch the investiture document is being read, and next to this figure the Marshal of Franconia again makes an appearance with the Franconian ducal sword. Tiepolo signed the picture on the bottom left: GIO.BTTA.TIEPOLO 1752).

The sun god Apollo conducts the allegory of Burgundy to the Genius Imperii (section), ceiling fresco by G. B. Tiepolo in the Imperial Hall

The side frescoes show two historical scenes illustrating the mutual dependency and the relationship of trust between the episcopal principality of Würzburg and the Holy Roman Empire of the German Nation. While the secular power, the kneeling emperor, profited from the legitimation by the church of his second marriage, the prince of the church, the kneeling bishop, benefited from imperial acknowledgement of his ducal privileges. The painting in the ceiling panel shifts the events to a higher allegorical plane. On an altar-like throne sits the youthful allegory of the 'Genius Imperii', in other words the Empire, with Fame circling above him and dignitaries surrounding him with waving banners and the eagle of the Holy Roman Empire. The sun god Apollo approaches from the right in a magnificent quadriga, bringing him the rich County of Burgundy in the allegory of a bride. High above him flies Hymen, the god of marriage, bearing a lighted torch, and in front of the throne is a putto with the Franconian ducal sword. On the right Venus, Ceres and Bacchus observe the scene from a bank of clouds.

Page with sunshade, fresco by G. B. Tiepolo above the moulding in the Imperial Hall

The allegories and virtues in the lunette caps, painted green in green against a coffered gold ground, were probably largely the work of Giovanni Battista's son Giovanni Domenico Tiepolo. He also created the three oil paintings above the doors, which illustrate the mutual relationship between eccelesiastical and secular power with scenes from the ancient world. They show 'Emperor Constantine as the conqueror of Licinius and protector of the church', 'Emperor Justinian as law-giver' and 'St Ambrose preventing Emperor Theodosius from entering a church because of the blood bath in Thessaloniki'.

Emperor Justinian as lawgiver, sopraporta by Domenico Tiepolo in the Imperial Hall

This room, designed by Balthasar Neumann as the high point in the sequence of halls beginning with the Vestibule, is perfectly lit all the way up into the vault by the large lunette cap windows. The coloured or gilded architectural elements and ornamentation of Antonio Bossi gives the hall its elegant decoration as well as an effervescent lightness. Tiepolo finally transformed the entire upper half of the room into an illusionistic picture sphere. Pages, musicians and soldiers swarm out of the side frescoes above the main cornice on the long sides and the heavenly sphere of the ceiling fresco spills over into the room with the cloud on the bottom right, making a single entity of the picture and the room. The result is a sublimely harmonious, perfect synthesis of the arts.

Southern Imperial Apartments

ROOMS **6** TO **10**

*Writing cabinet
by K. M. Mattern,
1742 (Room 6)*

Like the imperial halls, imperial apartments are a typical
feature of German Baroque palaces. In addition to the ruler's own rooms, most of the electoral and ecclesiastical
residences, as well as many of the larger monasteries, had
sumptuously furnished state apartments, which as the
very best guest apartments were kept ready for a possible
visit by the emperor and with their picture programme
alluded to this function (imperial portraits, representations of the 'good regime' and of the virtues etc.). The
Imperial Apartments in the Würzburg Residence take up
the whole garden front on either side of the Imperial Hall.
Balthasar Neumann came back from Paris in 1723 with
the idea of producing a single magnificent enfilade with
all the doors arranged successively on the same axis to
give an uninterrupted view from end to end of the 169-m
suite. To achieve this he had to place the doors on the
short sides of the Imperial Hall not in the central axis but
close to the windows. The Southern Imperial Apartments
were decorated and furnished in 1740–1744 under Prince-
Bishop Friedrich Carl von Schönborn, who was involved
down to the last detail in the decision-making. Influenced
by his period of office as Imperial Vice-Chancellor in Vienna, he engaged numerous decorative artists whose work
reflected the Viennese Imperial Baroque style. Rudolf
Byss, the court painter who was born in Chur, functioned
as a kind of artistic director and also did some of the
painting himself, together with his pupils Johann Thalhofer and Anton Joseph Högler. The most important art-

ists were the brilliant stucco-worker from Porto near Lugano, Antonio Bossi, and the Vienna-trained Würzburg sculptor Johann Wolfgang van der Auwera, who also made drawings for the room decoration. The carvings and furniture were produced by the sculptor Ferdinand Hund from Upper Swabia and Georg Adam Guthmann together with his three brothers from Lower Franconia. The court potter and porcelain maker Dominikus Eder provided the stoves, Georg Oegg, the gifted court locksmith from Tyrol, was responsible for the wrought-iron work.

In 1945 the Imperial Apartments were destroyed by fire. The stucco ceilings and frescoes, as well as part of the wall decoration, succumbed to the flames, and some of the finest examples of Rococo interior decoration in Germany were lost. All the movable furnishings and some of the fixed decorations had however been moved to a safe place. The ceiling stucco-work was reconstructed in most of the rooms on the basis of old photos. The decision that was taken in the 1960s to replace the destroyed oil paintings let into the ceilings with a series of pictures by Antonio Bellucci created in around 1715 for Elector Palatine Johann Wilhelm's Bensberg Palace, actually runs counter to present conservational principles. These originals (on loan from the Bavarian State Painting Collections), which were adjusted to fit with extra side pieces, however play a very important role in recreating the overall room atmosphere.

6 ANTECHAMBER OF THE SOUTHERN IMPERIAL APARTMENTS

As an antechamber, this room has a relatively modest interior, which was completed in 1740–1744. The wall panelling is made of oak with simple rectangular fields framed by gilded beading, and the only seating was in the form of benches. Both the wall panelling and the carved and gilded frames of the pier mirrors were destroyed in the fire of

1945 and had to be reconstructed. One of the original gilded frames of the pier mirrors, carved in the Early Rococo style by Georg Adam Guthmann as early as 1736, was actually made for another room in the Residence. The stucco-work on the ceilings by Antonio Bossi, in white on a light-grey ground, has also been reconstructed. The original ceiling painting by Anton Clemens Lünenschloß 'Departure of the military to capture a castle', dating from 1738, has been replaced by the oil painting 'Thank-offering', by Antonio Bellucci from around 1715. As well as the furniture and tapestries, the sopraportas with their carved gilded frames are also part of the original decoration. They are the work of Giovanni Antonio Pellegrini: 'Hannibal swearing eternal enmity against Rome' and 'The Sacrifice of Polyxena'. The original magnificent porcelain stove, the work of the Würzburg court potter and porcelain maker Dominikus Eder from Vienna, which like the mirror frames had been transferred to this room from the First Episcopal Apartment, has been replaced by a smaller stove of the same provenance (Austria, c. 1740, possibly from Eder's circle). The lower section of Antonio Bossi's stucco-work in the stove niches has been partially reconstructed.

Tapestries: 3 Brussels tapestries from the Alexander Cycle from cartoons by Charles Le Brun made by the manufactory of Jan Frans van den Hecke, after 1700: 'Alexander the Great crossing the Granicus' (rear wall), joined in around 1745 by a connecting piece of tapestry by Andreas Pirot to 'Battle at Arbela – Darius flees from Alexander' (entrance wall); also 'Battle at Arbela – pursuit of the fleeing Persians' (exit wall).

Furnishings: Writing Cabinet ('Trisur') with rich marquetry (walnut, ebony, rosewood, mother-of-pearl, ivory, brass). Masterpiece by the Würzburg cabinet-maker Karl Maximilian Mattern, who worked on this splendid but heavily-proportioned

Audience Room of the Southern Imperial Apartments (Room 7)

piece of furniture in 1742. The gilded carvings as well as the designs for the brass engravings are by Johann Wolfgang van der Auwera. On the door is the coat of arms of Prince-Bishop Friedrich Carl von Schönborn with the imperial crown, which as Prince-Bishop of Bamberg too he was entitled to include ■ Magnificent longcase clock with rich marquetry (walnut, mahogany, rosewood) and Schönborn coat of arms by Karl Maximilian Mattern, Würzburg, 1741. The gilded Rococo carvings on the base and top are by Georg Adam Guthmann, the remarkable clockwork by horologer Urban Schmidt, Würzburg (clock face signed: 'VRBANNS SCHMIT IN WURTZBURG Fecit') ■ 2 console tables, carved, brown with gold, by Georg Adam Guthmann, 1742 ■ 4 and 2 banquettes, carved, brown with gold, by Johann Wolfgang van der Auwera, Würzburg, after

1750. The remarkable tapestry coverings (flowers, fruit and rocaille work on a dark blue background) are from French models, Würzburg, Pirot Manufactory, after 1750 ■ 4 and 2 sconces, two-armed, gilded bronze, by the court locksmith Georg Oegg, Würzburg, c. 1745 ■ 2 glass arm chandeliers with coloured glass flowers; one of them by court glassmaker Johann Michael Faller, Würzburg, 1760 (partially reconstructed); one a modern copy.

▣ AUDIENCE ROOM OF THE SOUTHERN IMPERIAL APARTMENTS

By comparison with the Antechamber, the décor of the room has a dignified splendour simply through the exquisite walnut panelling with carved and gilded frames, inset with dark burl wood. The highlight of this decoration is the outstanding original Rococo carving with its unique variety of forms in the gilded frames of the fireplace and pier mirrors created by Ferdinand Hund from 1740. The rocaille ornamentation seems to detach itself from the background and ripple out into the room. The stucco-work by Antonio Bossi on the ceiling, which is also gilded, has been reconstructed. The oil painting by Antonio Bellucci, 'The three ages of the ruler' c. 1715 is a replacement for the destroyed ceiling painting by the Bamberg court painter Johann Joseph Scheubel the Elder, 'The destruction of a robber baron's castle by Rudolph von Habsburg,' which was an allusion to the function of this suite of rooms as an imperial guest apartment. The fireplace of violet- and agate-coloured marble in the French Régence style with the Schönborn coat of arms on the cast-iron chimney-plate is part of the original decoration, as are also the sopraporta paintings, complete with their carved Rococo frames. They depict 'Venus, Cupid and Charis', Venetian, c. 1600, and 'The building of Noah's Ark' by Giacomo Bassano. The large stove in the Régence style by the Würzburg court potter and porcelain maker Dominikus Eder from Vienna has been replaced by a smaller, South German Rococo stove in white and gold, c. 1755. The stucco of the stove niches has been reconstructed.

Tapestries: 4 Brussels tapestries, 3 of them from the Alexander Cycle, from cartoons by Charles Le Brun: 'Triumphal procession of Alexander the Great in Babylon' and 'Alexander's magnanimity toward the family of Darius' (rear wall) from the manufactory of Jan Frans van den Hecke, after 1700; 'Alexander's victory over King Poros of India (Part a): Prisoners' procession' with the coat of arms of Prince-Bishop Johann Philipp von Greiffenclau (r. 1699–1719), from the manufactory of Geraert Peemans, c. 1700 (entrance wall, cf. Rooms 14 and 15). 'Wedding of Zenobia' (exit wall) also from the manufactory of G. Peemans, but of earlier date, c. 1660.

Furnishings: Writing cabinet with rich marquetry (walnut, ebony, rosewood) and the initials FC of the Prince-Bishop of Würzburg, Friedrich Carl von Schönborn (r. 1729–1746); Würzburg, c. 1740, possibly by Franz Benedikt Schlecht, the gilded carvings by G. A. Guthmann, the gilded bronze fittings by Georg Oegg (on loan from the Bayerische Landesbank) ■ Fireplace screen with magnificent gilded Rococo carving, Würzburg, probably by Johann Wolfgang van der Auwera, 1742–1744 ■ 4 console tables, 2 on the window piers, carved, brown with gold, by Georg Adam Guthmann, 1742, the 2 others, carved and gilded, by Johann Wolfgang van der Auwera, Würzburg, c. 1744 ■ 4 armchairs (3+1 copy), carved, gilded, by Johann Wolfgang van der Auwera, Würzburg, 1741. Old coverings with coarse and petit point embroidery on canvas ■ 2 tabourets, carved, gilt, Würzburg, c. 1740 ■ 2 crystal chandeliers, one from Vienna, c. 1750, the other a modern copy ■ 4 two-armed and 2 three-armed sconces, gilded bronze, Würzburg (probably by the court locksmith Georg Oegg), c. 1740–1745 ■ 2 andirons and a set of 3 fire irons, Würzburg, c. 1750.

Maria Theresia spent the night of 20 September 1745 in this room on her way to the coronation of her husband Franz I Stephan, who had been elected German-Roman emperor a week before. She preferred to sleep in the camp bed she had brought with her rather than in the bed provided. The wall decoration was completed in 1738–1741 from designs by the elderly court painter Rudolf Byss, who died at the end of 1738. His pupils Johann Thalhofer and Anton Joseph Högler finished the ceiling painting on a ground of polished plaster that he had begun. In keeping with the function of the room as the guest bedroom for the emperor, its themes are night, sleep and dreams. The two main scenes depict the King of Bohemia being summoned in a dream to defend the church and the sleeping emperor being summoned to take up the fight against faithlessness. While the first ceiling was destroyed in 1945 and reconstructed from photos in 1964, the wall panelling and the doors of light ('blond') walnut are original. The small oil paintings on wooden panels inserted in the panelling were also created by Thalhofer and Högler, assisted by Georg Anton Urlaub. Depicted in the wainscot panelling are dwarfs, some of which are caricatures, animals and children at play, while the paintings in the window jambs and door panels show figures in contemporary costume. The carved cartouche-like frames were cast from tin from designs by Byss and models by Ferdinand Hund and gilded (only the frames on the door panels are carved). They resemble gilded bronze, but were much cheaper to produce. Above the doors and pier mirrors are five paintings with allegories of the virtues which are possibly the work of Rudolf Byss. The pyramid-shaped tiled stove by the Würzburg court potter and porcelain maker Dominikus Eder from Vienna, which was destroyed in 1945, has been

replaced by another stove of the same stylistic provenance. The blue-grey stucco marble and the gilded stucco in the stove niches have been partially reconstructed.

Tapestries: 3 tapestries from the Würzburg manufactory of Andreas Pirot, c. 1740–1745, with scenes from the carnival in Venice and the commedia dell'arte, from cartoons by Johann Joseph Scheubel the Elder: 'Carnival procession on St Mark's Square in Venice', signed 'A:PIROT.V:W:' (entrance wall, cf. Room 10), 'Banquet in a kiosk' (rear wall), 'Banquet in the open air' (exit wall, cf. Room 10).

Doors of the Venetian Room with gilded tin decorations and paintings, c. 1740 (Room 8)

Furnishings: 2 console tables, carved, brown with gold, Würzburg, c. 1740 (workshop of Georg Adam Guthmann) ▪ Gaming table, carved, gilded, glass top with reverse glass painting, design and frame by Johann Wolfgang van der Auwera, Würzburg, c. 1745 ▪ 4 armchairs, carved, blue with gold, German, c. 1741. Old coverings with gros point and petit point embroidery on canvas ▪ 4 sconces, two-armed, gilded bronze, Würzburg, 1742, by Georg Oegg ▪ Glass arm chandelier with coloured pendeloques and flowers, Johann Michael Faller, Würzburg, c. 1750 (partially reconstructed).

▣ MIRROR CABINET OF THE SOUTHERN IMPERIAL APARTMENTS

The wall decoration of the Mirror Cabinet, created in 1740–1745 and the most sumptuous room in the Residence from the time of Prince-Bishop Friedrich Carl von Schönborn (r. 1729–1746), was completely destroyed in the bombing raids of 1945. Based on a preserved mirror fragment, numerous photographs and a watercolour in opaque paint by Georg Dehn (c. 1870–1873), from 1979–1987 it was however possible to reproduce the decoration of all the enclosing walls using the old techniques. This reconstruction, together with the preserved furnishings,

gives visitors an idea of the overwhelming effect once created by what is perhaps the most original work of interior
decoration in the Würzburg Rococo style.

Mirror cabinets are a feature of numerous German Baroque
and Rococo palaces. They are usually panelled rooms
with inset mirrors, carvings and stucco-work, where porcelain was frequently displayed. The walls of the Würzburg Mirror Cabinet, however, were clad entirely in glass
panels, which were prepared on the back using a special
technique of reverse glass painting: either the paintings
were made on the partially recessed mirror ground, or
drawings were engraved into a gold ground that was applied to the back of the mirror, and then underlaid with
dark varnish paint. By this means, instead of displaying

Oriental porcelain figures in front of the mirrors as was customary, numerous exotic figures and scenes were incorporated directly into the mirror.

For many years Prince-Bishop Friedrich Carl von Schönborn took an intense personal interest in every detail of the decoration of the Mirror Cabinet. It is possible that he decided in favour of reverse glass painting following a suggestion by Balthasar Neumann, who had earlier recommended the same technique for the panels of the wainscot in the adjacent gallery. The final concept for the Mirror Cabinet was established at a meeting in 1740 to which Friedrich Carl invited not only Balthasar Neumann, but also the court sculptor Johann Wolfgang van der Auwera and the stucco-worker Antonio Bossi.

The stuccoing of the dome vault, completed in 1741, is one of Antonio Bossi's finest achievements. In the corner panels of the vault are small scenes showing the four continents represented by allegorical female figures. In the middle are four genii bearing a huge curved mirror aloft. The figures are all in colour, some of which has a metallically iridescent sheen. The otherwise fully gilded, graceful stucco ornamentation that completely covers the white background of the vault is given further colour accents with putti, heads, flowers, dragons and birds. Even the heavy gilded draperies with small mirrors set into them that billow over the moulding below seem to echo the flowing movement of the entire ornamental scheme.

The versatile court sculptor and graphic artist Johann Wolfgang van der Auwera designed the figures and the ornamental decoration of the mirror walls, as well as the richly carved tables with painted glass tops. The Byss disciples Johann Thalhofer and Anton Högler, together with Georg Anton Urlaub assisted by his father Georg Sebastian Urlaub and his brother Georg Christian Urlaub produced the paintings in 1741–1744 (reconstructed by Wolfgang Lenz). Except for the black marble fireplace and the

View of the Mirror Cabinet before destruction, watercolour by Georg Dehn, c. 1870

white wainscot and double doors, which also have mirrors set into them (the two wings of the doors on the north side are original), the walls consist entirely of mirror and glass panels, most of them irregularly curved, with ornamental gilded stucco-work concealing the joins.

The apparent dissolution of all spatial boundaries through the reproduction effect of the mutually reflecting mirror walls has an initially confusing effect. The symmetry and the colour gradation of the individual glass surfaces only gradually emerge as the essential structuring elements of the wall design. Leaving aside the unpainted mirrors, the reverse glass paintings can roughly be divided into four pattern/ground colour combinations: gold on white, multicoloured on white, multicoloured on a mirror ground and gold on blue.

The four curved elongated oval mirrors, to the left and right of the fireplace and on the side walls, which are each divided into three sections, are the largest empty mirror surfaces. A few smaller pairs of similarly unpainted mirrors are located above the fireplace, on the opposite window pier and in the remaining unequally dimensioned parts of the wall by the windows. Around the frames of the four large three-part wall mirrors are two pairs of diagonally aligned golden atlantes on a white ground; continuing outwards from these figures are four coloured ornamental panels surrounded with floral decoration, each featuring a female bust. A further ensemble of pictures grouped cruciformly around the centre mirror and painted in a variety of colours on an uncoloured mirror ground, features Chinese figures: below, noble Chinese, most being carried by their servants and accompanied by a retinue; above, a Chinese man and a Chinese woman worshiping an idol; to the left and right of each centre mirror and separated by it a seated noble Chinese couple. The remaining glass panels have a (probably originally even more brilliant) lapis lazuli blue ground, inset with exotic hunting scenes, jugglers,

View of the Mirror Cabinet, reconstructed in 1979–1987

acrobats and musicians primarily in a gold colour, with occasional brightly-coloured birds or fruit. The golden plants and tendrils painted on the blue glass seem to merge with the stucco-work covering the joins between the mirrors, so that the walls appear to be covered by a fine web of golden tendrils, which simultaneously frames and connects the individual scenes.

The walls of the two window niches depict male and female singers, dancers and musicians. The wainscot mirrors on the window side are painted with eight animal scenes that probably represent the virtues and vices, and on the window pier is a Chinese tea party. In the middle wainscot mirrors of the side walls are the coat of arms and initials of Friedrich Carl von Schönborn, flanked by two allegories of the seasons. The wainscot mirrors of the fireplace wall feature allegories of the four elements.

The plain panelled parquetry of the floor has been reconstructed in its original form, as has also the black marble fireplace with the Schönborn coat of arms. The inset iron chimney plates, with wrought-iron tendril ornamentation that also contains Friedrich Carl's initials, are however from the original fireplace.

Armchair with embroidered covering, c. 1741 (Room 9)

Furnishings: 2 console tables, frames with inlaid mirror pieces, carved and gilded, glass table tops with reverse glass painting. Design and frame by Johann Wolfgang van der Auwera, Würzburg, c. 1745 ■ Gaming table, carved, gilded, glass top with reverse glass painting. Design and frame by Johann Wolfgang van der Auwera, Würzburg, c. 1745 ■ Fire screen with elegant, gilded carving in Régence

and Early Rococo styles, Würzburg, c. 1736, by Ferdinand
Hund (probably from the Second Episcopal Apartment in the
south block). On the front are the initials of Friedrich Carl von
Schönborn with the ducal hat in gold and silk embroidery (on
the back there was originally a vase with flowers in Savonnerie
technique) ■ 4 armchairs, carved, white with gold, German,
c. 1741. Old coverings with gros point and petit point embroidery on canvas ■ 2 East Asian porcelain dolls, early 18th century ■ 14 sconces (4 three-armed, 8 and 2 two-armed), gilded
bronze; 4 copies have been added to the preserved and restored
originals by Georg Oegg, Würzburg, c. 1745 ■ Glass arm
chandelier with coloured glass flowers, Venice, before 1756
(partially reconstructed).

▣ GALLERY OF THE SOUTHERN IMPERIAL
APARTMENTS

The art gallery, which takes up the five window axes at
the south end of the garden front, originally had a dome
vault that extended to the upper mezzanine. In 1740–1744
the room was splendidly decorated with stucco marble
under Balthasar Neumann and the walls were filled with
inset pictures surrounded by gilded stucco frames. At the
beginning of the 19th century, Grand Duke Ferdinand III
of Tuscany, who reigned from 1806 to 1814 as Grand
Duke of Würzburg, had the gallery divided into three
rooms (study, antechamber, boudoir) and completely re-
furnished along with the other Tuscany Rooms in the Empire style (see the exhibition in Room 13a–c). Since the
permanent wall furnishings of the Tuscany rooms were
completely destroyed by the bombing in 1945, however,
the current gallery, of which only the ground plan was
reconstructed, and in 1968–1969 was panelled in oak like
the South Antechamber, is based on the suite of rooms
created in the 18th century. The green silk wall covering
was replaced in 2015.

On the ceiling are three allegorical oil paintings by Antonio Bellucci, c. 1715, with 'The pursuit of happiness' in the middle, flanked by two 'Allegories of the young and successful ruler'. The sopraportas, Franconian work from the mid-18th century with carved gilt frames, are similarly not part of the original decoration. They depict scenes from ancient Roman history (virtues romanae): 'The victory of the Horatii over the Curatii' (entrance wall), 'Horatius pleads for his son, who has been sentenced to death' (rear wall on the left), 'Gaius Mucius Scaevola burning his own hand in front of Porsenna' (middle) and 'The suicide of Lucretia' (right).

Tapestries: 3 Brussels tapestries from the Würzburg manufactory of Andreas Pirot, c. 1749–1750, with scenes from the carnival in Venice and the commedia dell'arte, from cartoons by Johann Joseph Scheubel the Elder: 'Pantalone and Doctor Baloard' (entrance wall), 'Carnival procession on St Mark's Square in Venice' (rear wall left, cf. Room 8), 'Banquet in the open air' (rear wall right, cf. Room 8).

Paintings: Portraits of the eight prince-bishops of Würzburg since the Residence was begun (on the window piers from left to right and top to bottom): Johann Philipp Franz von Schönborn (r. 1719–1724), the founder of the Residence; Christoph Franz von Hutten (r. 1724–1729); Friedrich Carl von Schönborn (r. 1729–1746), who continued the project; Anselm Franz von Ingelheim (r. 1746–1749); Carl Philipp von Greiffenclau (r. 1749–1754), who brought in Tiepolo; Adam Friedrich von Seinsheim (r. 1755–1779), who completed the interior and the Court Garden; Franz Ludwig von Erthal (r. 1779–1795), and finally Georg Carl von Fechenbach, who was the last prince-bishop (from 1795–1802, then bishop until 1808).

Furnishings: 5 console tables, carved, brown with gold, the more elaborate of these are by Georg Adam Guthmann, the simpler ones from his workshop, c. 1735–1740 ▪ 3 glass arm chandeliers with coloured glass flowers (copies, cf. Room 6) ▪ Mirror, carved, gilded, Franconian, c. 1760 (probably by Johann Jakob Berg, Eichstätt).

11 MEMORIAL ROOM IN REMEMBRANCE OF THE DESTRUCTION IN 1945

This room contains an exhibition documenting the massive damage to the Residence resulting from the air raid in 1945 and the vital action taken by the American officer of the Monuments and Fine Arts Section John D. Skilton to save it.

12 AND 13 DOCUMENTATION OF THE RECONSTRUCTION AFTER 1945

Documentation of the reconstruction of the Residence after 1945 and the reconstruction of the Mirror Cabinet from 1979 to 1987.

13a-c EXHIBITION 'AT HOME WITH THE GRAND DUKE'

In these rooms some of the furnishing preserved from the apartment of Grand Duke Ferdinand III of Tuscany, which was destroyed in 1945, is on display. The Habsburg Ferdinand III (born 1769, died 1824), a grandson of Maria Theresia and brother of the German-Roman emperor Franz II, was driven out of Tuscany by French troops and received as compensation first Salzburg, and then, in 1805 as a result of the Treaty of Pressburg, the secularized bishopric of Würzburg. He took up occupancy of the Residence on 1 May 1806 as Grand Duke of Würzburg. For eight years he reigned here under the watchful eye of the French before he was able return to his hereditary grand duchy in Florence in 1814.

Ferdinand III of Tuscany, who came to Würzburg as a widower with young children, had three apartments redesigned in the modern Empire style for himself, his future second wife and his two daughters. For reasons of economy, the architect entrusted with the task, Nicolas-Alexandre Salins de Montfort, was instructed to take over the existing ground plans of three suites of rooms on the main floor more or less as they were and only redesign their appointments.

The suite of rooms for the grand duke (Apartment I) was created in the cour d'honneur and city wing of the south block. In what was originally called the Second Episcopal Apartment and was occupied by Friedrich Carl von Schönborn in 1737, the new interior replaced the Baroque furnishing which would have looked 'old-fashioned' and was probably already very worn out. The suite intended for the future grand duchess in the Court Garden wing of the south block (Appartment II) began in the Southern Oval immediately adjacent to the Court Chapel and extended – with the three new rooms in place of the gallery in the south-eastern corner – as far as the Mirror Cabinet. This suite of rooms was finished first and was initially occupied by the grand duke himself, since Ferdinand did not remarry until after his return to Tuscany. A third, more modest suite of rooms (Apartment III) was furnished in the cour d'honneur wing of the north block as an apartment for Ferdinand's two young daughters.

The Tuscany Rooms were designed in the contemporary Empire style by the interior architect Nicolas-Alexandre Salins de Montfort (1753–1839), who had trained in France. His closest associate was the Frankfurt upholsterer Ludwig Daniel Philipp Rumpf (1762–1845), a specialist in furniture manufacture and furnishing textiles. Suites of furniture were also supplied from Frankfurt by the cabinet-maker Johann Valentin Raab (1777–1839) and the workshop of Philipp Carl Hildebrand (1753–1805) who had died shortly beforehand. Most of the bronze work and clocks were obtained from France, and the glass chandeliers came from Dresden.

All of the permanent wall decoration of the Tuscany Rooms was destroyed in the fire following the bombardment of Würzburg in 1945. Only the grotesques painted in the Music or Dining Room in the Southern Oval (now the 'Tuscany Hall' in the university area) could be restored and partially reconstructed; this work was finished in 1965. The other rooms were incorporated into the Martin von Wagner Museum and the Graphics Collection of Würzburg University, into the new Gallery (Room 10), of which the original ground plan was restored, and the 'Charlotte Corridor' (Room 40) and its adjoining rooms. Much of the moveable furnishing – primarily seating ensembles – had however been saved. The selection of furniture on display here provides a record of the original Tuscany rooms and their appointments as one of the most important examples of an Empire-style interior. A particular favourite with the public is the carousel that Grand Duke Ferdinand initially installed for his children in Werneck Palace.

ROOM 13a

Painting: Grand Duke Ferdinand III of Tuscany, German, c. 1810.

Furniture from the Guard Room: Chairs and tabourets (stools), carved, German, c. 1809 and later.

Furniture from the Cabinet of Crown Prince Ludwig (I) of Bavaria: Sofa, chairs and fire screen with mahogany varnish and gilded bronze and brass appliques, probably English, c. 1792, coverings after 1814 ■ Chandelier, supported by the goddess Nike, wood, metal, painted to look like bronze and partially gilded, German, 1807–1808.

Selection of further unrestored Tuscany furniture.

Furnishing from the Large Salon: Divan (in two parts), bergères (wing chairs), armchairs, chairs, tabourets (stools) and fire screen, gilded beech, red half-silk lampas with gold patterns (replaced before 1898), Johann Valentin Raab, Frankfurt am Main, c. 1807–1809 ■ Pendule (bracket clock) of gilded bronze with the figures of Iphigenie and Orestes, yellow marble pedestal (reconstructed), probably by Pierre-François Feuchère, Paris, c. 1817 ■ Cupid and Psyche candelabra, gilded bronze, yellow marble pedestal (reconstructed), Pierre-François Feuchère, Paris, 1817 ■ Andiron with cornucopia, gilded bronze, yellow marble pedestal (reconstructed), Pierre-François Feuchère, Paris, 1817.

Furnishing from the Living Room: Armchairs, chairs and tabourets (stools) painted white and partially gilded, red atlas silk with velvet decoration, German, after 1810 ■ Chandelier with Egyptian masks, beech, painted green and gold, German (?), 1807–1809.

Candelabras from various Tuscany Rooms: Candelabra with the winged goddess Nike, carved, painted green and gold, German (?), c. 1807–1808 ■ Candelabra with Egyptian woman, painted green and gold, German (?), c. 1807–1808 ■ Candelabra, consisting of gueridons and girandoles, carved, painted green and gold, German (?), after 1811 ■ Candelabra, consisting of gueridons and girandoles, carved, gilded, French (?), c. 1810.

Carousel with accessories, made for the children of Grand Duke Ferdinand (on loan from the Wittelsbach Compensation Fund, Munich): Children's carousel with two horses and two seats, wood painted in colour, metal, also partly coloured, leather, horsehair, Germany, c. 1806 ■ 2 columns with heads ■

Replacement noses for the heads (papier mâché) ▪ Column with an arm holding a snake ▪ Rings for the ring tilt game ▪ Throwing game with arrows and target ▪ Throwing game with balls and a target with holes in it ▪ Stand with three lances ▪ Accessory case.

Furnishing from the Boudoir: Sofa, armchair, chairs, tabourets (stools) and table, maple and beech, silver fittings, violet silk lampas with a gold-coloured pattern (replaced), Johann Valentin Raab, Frankfurt am Main, 1809 ▪ Psyche (standing mirror), walnut, maple and mahogany varnish, silver and gilded brass fittings, mirror glass, yellow silk taffeta covering on the back, Johann Valentin Raab, Frankfurt am Main, 1809 ▪ Brass chandelier, gilded, French, after 1816 ▪ 2 door wings, mahogany, fruitwood, partially silvered, gilded or painted, mirror glass, German, c. 1809 ▪ Pendule (bracket clock) 'Telemachus's chariot', gilded bronze, enamel, Jean-André Reiche (design), Denière et Matelin (production), Paris, 1810–1815 (new acquisition).

Children's carousel and furniture from the boudoir of the Tuscany period 1806–1814

Northern Imperial Apartments

In 1743–1744, as the work on the Southern Imperial
Apartments was nearing completion, the interior of the
Northern Imperial Apartments was begun while Prince-
Bishop Friedrich Carl von Schönborn (r. 1729–1746) was
still in power. Because of the imperial election in autumn
1745, Schönborn hurried it along to have guest rooms
available, even if initially only in a simplified form. The
first four rooms only acquired their final character as
magnificent state apartments under Prince-Bishop Carl
Philipp von Greiffenclau (r. 1749–1754), who had the
stucco-work on the walls gilded and more furniture installed. It was not until after the Seven Years' War under
Prince-Bishop Adam Friedrich von Seinsheim (r. 1755–
1779) that the suite of 'ordinari' guest room that goes up
to the Rennweg on the north side, where Tiepolo and his
sons resided from 1750 to 1753, was furnished in the tran-
sitional style between Late Rococo and Neoclassicism.
The last room was only completed in 1772.

The first rooms of the Northern Imperial Apartments are
already very different in character from their southern
counterparts, as in the meantime the Würzburg artists and
craftsmen had moved on from Viennese Régence decoration to Würzburg Rococo. Thus, as in the Mirror Cabinet,
the panelling was painted white instead of being left in its
original colour, and the gilded carvings on the fireplace
and pier mirrors were replaced by equally lavish stucco-
work. The dominant colours are no longer deep browns
and gold but light colours, with white combined with

*Writing cabinet
by K. M. Mattern
and G. A. Guth-
mann, c. 1745
(Room 15)*

105

gold. In the old inventories these rooms were in fact listed as 'White Rooms'. Against the background of these light and delicate rococo decorations, the High Baroque tapestries are almost too dramatic and intensely coloured. As the coats of arms show, these Brussels tapestries from the manufactory of Geraert Peemans were produced under Prince-Bishop Johann Philipp von Greiffenclau (r. 1699–1719), the uncle of Carl Philipp. These works, which even then were highly valuable, were commissioned before the Residence was built for the fortress of Marienberg.

During the restoration that was completed in 1974, the stucco-work on all the ceiling panels had to be replaced. Most of the stucco decoration in the cavetto mouldings, on the walls and around the sopraportas and mirrors is original, likewise most of the sopraporta paintings.

14 ANTECHAMBER OF THE NORTHERN IMPERIAL APARTMENTS

The paneling, painted white, is decorated only with plain rectangles surrounded by gilded frames. In 1744 Antonio Bossi filled the corner fields of the pure white ceiling stucco-work with allegories of the four elements (reconstructed). One year later he added the magnificent stucco decoration featuring Venus and Endymion on the fireplace mirror (original, partially reconstructed) and the window piers (reconstructed) in the flamboyant forms that characterized his late style. The original ceiling painting by A. C. Lünenschloß, 'The building of Würzburg Cathedral' (1741), which was destroyed by fire in 1945, has been replaced by an oil painting by Antonio Bellucci entitled 'The judgement of Paris on Mount Ida with Romulus and Remus' dating from 1715. The paintings and decoration surrounding the sopraportas are original: 'Genre piece', probably by Jan Cossiers (entrance wall); 'Mars and Venus', Flemish, 17th century (exit wall). In

place of the magnificent faience stove by the Würzburg potter and porcelain maker Dominikus Eder from Vienna dating from 1735, which was destroyed in 1945, is a white-and-gold Viennese Rococo stove made in around 1760. The black marble fireplace has a gilded cartouche with the Schönborn coat of arms.

Antechamber of the Northern Imperial Apartments with a tapestry by G. Peemans, c. 1700

Tapestries: 3 Brussels tapestries from the Alexander Cycle with the coat of arms of Prince-Bishop Johann Philipp von Greiffen-clau (r. 1699–1719) by Geraert Peemans, c. 1700: 'Alexander's victory over King Poros of India (Part b): Prisoners' procession' (entrance wall), 'Battle at Arbela / Darius flees from Alexan-der' (rear wall), 'Alexander's victory over King Poros of India (Part d): Alexander's retinue' (exit wall, cf. Rooms 7 and 15).

Furnishings: 2 console tables, carved, gilded, Würzburg, c. 1745–1750 (possibly by Ferdinand Hund) ■ 5 banquettes (4+1), carved, white with gold, by Andreas Michael Dietrich. The remarkable tapestry coverings (flowers and rocaille ornamentation on a white ground) are from the Würzburg manufactory of Andreas Pirot, c. 1752 ■ Lidded vase, octagonal, with Foo dog, Japanese, 18th century ■ Huge blue-and-white vase, Delft, 17th century ■ 6 sconces, two-armed, gilded bronze, Würzburg, c. 1745, by the court locksmith Georg Oegg ■ 2 glass arm chandeliers with coloured glass flowers (copies, cf. Room 6) ■ 2 andirons and set of 3 fire irons, Würzburg, c. 1750.

Magnificent clock by L. Hoys, Bamberg, 1750 (Room 15)

▣ AUDIENCE ROOM OF THE NORTHERN IMPERIAL APARTMENTS

The wood panelling is white with carved gilded ornamental frames. The white ceiling stucco decoration by Antonio Bossi dating from 1745 has been reconstructed, but most of the partially gilded stucco-work decorating the cavetto mouldings, the pier mirrors and the sopraportas and window niches is original. On the pier mirror is the white polished figure of Fama with attributes of prince-bishop rulership. Small fragments of mirror are set into Bossi's brilliant rocaille ornamentation. The ceiling painting by A. C. Lünenschloß 'The suppression of insurgent peasants by the Würzburg prince-bishop in 1525', destroyed in 1945, has been replaced by an oil painting by Antonio Bellucci dating from 1715 entitled 'Allegory of the princely patronage of the arts' (The liberation of Mercury by Art and Science). The two paintings in the sopraportas are original: 'The child Moses trampling on Pharaoh's crown' (entrance wall) and 'Susanna and the Elders' (exit wall), both by G. A. Pellegrini. In place of the splendid faience stove by the Würzburg court potter and porcelain maker Dominikus Eder from Vienna (1735), which was destroyed in 1945, there is a white-and-gold Viennese Rococo stove dating from around 1760.

Audience Room of the Northern Imperial Apartments (Room 15)

Tapestries: 3 Brussels tapestries from the Alexander Cycle with the coat of arms of the Würzburg prince-bishop Johann Philipp von Greiffenclau (r. 1699–1719) by Geraert Peemans, c. 1700: 'Alexander's victory over King Poros of India (Part c): The wounded Poros before Alexander' (entrance wall, cf. Rooms 7 and 14), 'Alexander's triumphal procession in Babylon' (rear wall), 'Alexander's magnanimity towards the family of Darius' (exit wall).

Furnishings: 2 differing console tables, carved, white with gold, Würzburg, c. 1750, by the court sculptor Andreas Michael Dietrich ■ Writing cabinet, inlaid (grained walnut, ivory, rosewood, tin) and carved, a masterpiece by the Würzburg cabinetmaker Karl Maximilian Mattern, with the gilded carvings probably by Georg Adam Guthmann, Würzburg, c. 1745 ■

Suite of seating furniture (1 sofa, 2 armchairs, 2 upholstered chairs), white with gold, carved, Würzburg, 1751, by the court sculptor Andreas Michael Dietrich. Remarkable old Strassbourg tapestry coverings with floral patterns on a white ground ■ Longcase clock, Würzburg, c. 1750–1760, clock face signed 'Langschwert Wirtzburg' ■ Bracket clock with music mechanism (6 melodies and 9 chimes), by Leopold Hoys, signed: 'LEOP.HOYS 1750 Bamberg' ■ 2 sconces, two-armed, gilded bronze, Würzburg, c. 1745, by Georg Oegg ■ Crystal chandelier, Vienna, c. 1750.

16 RED CABINET OF THE NORTHERN IMPERIAL APARTMENTS

The highly imaginative and delicate ceiling stucco-work by Antonio Bossi (partially reconstructed) dates from the first decoration phase. In addition to the emblems of the fine arts, music, the art of warfare and the sciences, naturalistic motifs were introduced such as trees, birds and busts. The gilded stucco frames of the pier mirrors and sopraportas are less elaborate than those of the previous rooms and the gilded carvings of the white doors and wainscot (reconstructed) look almost rigid. The sopraporta paintings are original: 'Moses in the bulrushes' by Sebastiano Mazzoni, Venice, c. 1650–1660 (entrance wall); 'Man with jewels', Italian, Caravaggio school (exit wall). The fireplace of blue-grey marble shows the Schönborn coat of arms, the cast iron stove plate dating from 1680 is from the fortress of Marienberg in Würzburg.

Paintings (on loan from the Bavarian State Collection of Paintings, Munich): Still life of flowers and fruit by Andreas Mattenheimer (1752–1810) ■ 2 still lifes with dead birds by Johann Albert Angermeyer (1674–1740) ■ Ideal landscape by Maximilian Joseph Schinnagl (1697–1762) ■ 2 small landscapes by Georg Friedrich Meyer (1735–1779).

Furnishings: 2 elegant, dainty console tables, carved, white with gold, Würzburg, c. 1745–1750 (probably by Johann Wolfgang van der Auwera) ■ 4 armchairs, carved, white with gold, coverings replaced, Würzburg, c. 1750 ■ 2 brightly painted sconces shaped like branches with foliage and flowers, wrought iron, painted in colour, Würzburg, 1751, by the court locksmith Georg Oegg ■ Crystal chandelier (partially reconstructed), Vienna, c. 1750 ■ Andirons and set of 3 fire irons, Würzburg, c. 1750.

17 GREEN DAMASK ROOM OF THE NORTHERN IMPERIAL APARTMENTS (RECEPTION ROOM)

The basic colour of this room, which was called the 'Green Damask Room' in the 18th century because of its wall covering at the time, is white, with relatively little gilding. The stucco decorations are on a light grey ground on the ceiling, and on a light green ground on the walls and mirrors. On the frame of the fireplace mirror are bizarre, white polished figures representing the four continents; while the pier mirrors are decorated with allegories of the Occident and Orient. The decoration is some of Antonio Bossi's best work and reflects the wildly extravagant style of his later years. The rocaille work, a riot of white and gold, sparkles with light reflected from the inserted mirror fragments. All of the stucco-work round the fireplace mirror and the sopraportas, and some of the work on the pier mirrors is original, whereas the window jamb and ceiling decoration has been reconstructed. In the centre of the ceiling is a relief of 'Franconia' surrounded by putti, busts and mythical creatures. While it is questionable whether the sopraportas 'Flora' and 'Bacchus', with frames carved by Andreas Dietrich c. 1745, can be attributed to Carlo Signani (Cignani), they are certainly the work of an Italian artist of the 17th or early 18th century. The blue-grey marble fireplace is decorated with the Schönborn coat of arms.

Paintings: The two state portraits of Emperor Karl VI (r. 1711–1740) and his wife Elisabeth Christine are probably copies by Johann Thalhofer of work by Johann Gottfried Auerbach. Their frames were carved by Georg Adam Guthmann and they originally hung above two fireplaces in the former Noblemen's Dining Hall, the subsequent Tuscany Hall.

Furnishings: 2 console tables, carved, white and gold on a green ground, Würzburg, c. 1745 (probably by Johann Wolfgang van der Auwera) ■ Pier table, white and gold on a green ground, carved, Würzburg, c. 1745, by Andreas Michael Dietrich ■ 4 upholstered chairs, carved, white and gold, Würzburg, probably by Andreas Michael Dietrich from a design by Byss (signed: M. R. Byss), 1751; old Strassbourg

Green Damask Room of the Northern Imperial Apartments (Room 17)

tapestry covers ■ 2 pot vases, Japanese (Imari), 18th century ■ 4 sconces in the form of branches with foliage, two-armed, painted in colour, Würzburg, c. 1750 ■ Crystal chandelier, partially reconstructed, Vienna, c. 1750 ■ 2 andirons with horses in levade and the Schönborn coat of arms, gilded bronze, Paris, c. 1720 ■ Set of 3 fire irons, c. 1750.

Wall clock with Chronos, originally with balancing mechanism; by M. Maerkel, Bamberg, 1764 (Room 18)

18 BEDROOM OF THE NORTHERN IMPERIAL APARTMENTS (NAPOLEON ROOM)

Emperor Napoleon, who stayed in Würzburg three times in 1806, 1812 and 1813 during the reign of Grand Duke Ferdinand III of Tuscany, slept in this room. The state beds and bedside tables from the Tuscany Rooms were installed here for his stay in 1812, when he was accompanied by his second wife Marie-Louise, a niece of Ferdinand. The room had also previously been used as a guest bedroom. The decoration and furnishing was interrupted by the Seven Years' War and was recommenced only in 1763. The Würzburg Rococo style was by then in its late phase, which rather surprisingly lasted right into the seventies. During the first stage of the decoration in around 1745, Antonio Bossi created the stucco-work around the ceiling panel; during the second stage in 1763, Friedrich Manger completed the gilded central section with dancing putti and a flower garland on a pink-toned ground, and all the stucco-work on the walls and in the window niches. The original wainscot only had stucco decoration, which has been reconstructed like that of the ceiling panel. The partially reconstructed faience stove with floral painting in burnt-in colours was supplied by Franz Paul Acker from Strassbourg in 1764. The sopraportas: 'Jupiter and Mercury' (signed in the bottom right-hand corner: 'Sanguinetti') and 'Mercury and Argus' were painted by Lazaro Maria Sanguinetti; 'Soldier and procuress' (rear wall) is by Dirk van Baburen.

Bedroom of the Northern Imperial Apartments, known as the Napoleon Room (Room 18)

Painting: The portrait of Pope Benedict XIV (r. 1740–1758) by Ignaz Stern the Younger originally hung 'in the prince-bishop's living room' of the Second Episcopal Apartment in 1778.

Furnishings: 2 state beds and 2 bedside tables, carved, gilded, by Johann Valentin Raab, 1809 (baldachin replaced) ■ 2 console-tables, carved, gilded, Würzburg, 1771–1772, by Daniel Köhler ■ Suite of seating furniture consisting of 1 corner sofa, 2 arm-chairs and 6 upholstered chairs, carved, gilded (covering replaced), Würzburg, 1771–1772, by Daniel Köhler ▪ Wall clock with Chronos, originally with balancing mechanism, by Martin Maerkel, Bamberg, c. 1764 ▪ 2 sconces, two-armed, gilded bronze, Würzburg, mid-18th century ▪ Crystal chandelier, Vienna, c. 1750.

19 FIRST GUEST ROOM OF THE NORTHERN IMPERIAL APARTMENTS (SOUPER ROOM)

Together with the Bedroom, this and the two following rooms form a self-contained apartment designed for the use of high-ranking visitors. The wall decoration consists entirely of white, partially gilded stucco-work. In the first decoration phase Antonio Bossi worked on the ceiling cove, in the second Friedrich Manger completed the wall and ceiling stucco-work in the style typical of the end of the Rococo period: the rocaille ornamentation is sparing and has been overtaken by naturalistic blossoms and foliate ornamentation. The frames no longer describe lively, asymmetrical curves, but have become either more rigid or fully rectangular. In the stucco-work above the window niches are the initials AF of Prince-Bishop Adam Friedrich von Seinsheim. The four reliefs above the mirrors and in the corner niches showing the deeds

Writing cabinet by A. Roentgen, c. 1768 (Room 19)

117

of ancient heroes were created by Antonio Petrolli in 1764–1765. The sopraportas (from left to right) are entitled as follows: 'Mars and Minerva', possibly a copy after Gerard de Lairesse; 'Night-piece' by Giacomo Bassano; 'Cupid and putti taking away arms', probably by Thomas Willeborts; 'Pastrycook', probably by Antonio Amorosi. Strassbourg faience stove with paintings in purple (Hercules scenes) by Franz Paul Acker, 1766 (stove and stucco-work partially reconstructed).

Tapestries: 2 Brussels tapestries from the manufactory of Jan Frans van den Hecke, Brussels, c. 1680, with representations of the four elements: 'Fire and earth', 'Air and water'.

Furnishings: 2 writing cabinets by Abraham Roentgen, Neuwied, c. 1765–1768, with rocaille work, flowers, fruits and birds in coloured marquetry. The one with two doors in the

Previous double page: First Guest Room of the Northern Imperial Apartments (Room 19)

Sofa, Franconian, c. 1765–1770 (Room 19)

120

lower section is known to have been in Würzburg since 1768 (ash, cedar, rosewood, etc.), the one with two drawers in the lower part was acquired in 1961 (oak, maple, amaranth, boxwood, birch, padauk etc.) ■ Console table, carved, white and gold, Franconian, c. 1750 (acquired in 1966) ■ Console table, carved, white and gold, Franconian, c. 1765–1770 ■ Outstanding suite of seating furniture (1 sofa, 6 upholstered chairs) in the Late Rococo style, gilded, carved, Franconian, c. 1765–1770. Old Savonnerie covers, 1770, from the manufactory of Peter Jesse in Heidelberg ■ Crystal chandelier, Vienna, c. 1740–1750 ■ 4 sconces, two-armed, gilded bronze, Würzburg, mid-18th century.

20 SECOND GUEST ROOM OF THE NORTHERN IMPERIAL APARTMENTS (TEA ROOM)

This room is an example of Late Würzburg Rococo. While some of the decoration reverts to the Régence style, rocaille ornamentation is increasingly less in evidence. The decorative frames are more solid, with no movement in them. The stucco decoration of the ceiling and walls, entirely in white and gold, is all the work of Materno and Ludovico Bossi and dates from 1766–1767. Above the mirrors are pairs of putti holding round paintings by the Bamberg court painter Nicolaus Treu: 'Comedian with mask' (entrance wall), 'Old man with hourglass and book' (rear wall), 'Money-counter' (exit wall) and 'St Joseph with the Infant Jesus' (copy, window wall). Above the doors and false doors are rectangularly framed sopraportas (comprehensively restored after war damage): 'Lady with violin (?)', French, 17th century, and 'Lady with faun playing a flute', Italian, 17th century (entrance wall); 'Lady with lute', possibly by Pietro de Liberi, and 'Lady at the spinet' (copy, exit wall). The fireplace is of blue-grey marble. The stucco decoration was partially reconstructed, while the elaborate inlaid floor was entirely replaced.

Furnishings: 3 console tables, originally by J. P. Wagner, 1768 (destroyed in 1945 and reconstructed from photos in 1997), carved, gilded, red marble tops ▪ Table, originally by F. Tietz, c. 1765 (destroyed in 1945 and reconstructed from photos), carved, gilded, red marble top ▪ Suite of seating furniture (2 sofas, 2 armchairs) in the Late Rococo style, gilded, carved, Würzburg, c. 1760, with replaced red damask covers ▪ Stove screen, carved and gilded, Würzburg, c. 1760 ▪ 8 sconces, two-armed, gilded bronze, Würzburg, mid-18th century ▪ Crystal chandelier, Vienna, 1750.

21 GREEN LACQUERED ROOM OF THE NORTHERN IMPERIAL APARTMENTS

As the corner room of the immense garden façade, the Green Lacquered Room, which was decorated in 1769–1772, is the final one in the Northern and Southern Imperial Apartments suite, which has a total length of 169 m. It is a unique room that perfectly reflects Late Würzburg Rococo and Early Neoclassicism. After the creative Mirror Cabinet in the Southern Imperial Apartments, this room is the most original if not the most important of the typical Würzburg Residence interiors. The particular atmosphere of the room is created by its luminous green, applied as a glaze on a silver ground to give the colour depth and an unusual translucent quality. The overall effect is heightened by the gilded stucco decorations in Late Rococo forms by Materno Bossi and the charming diversity of the colourful paintings showing landscapes, scenes with putti, clusters of blossom, butterflies, etc. The paintings in the cavetto mouldings and above the mirrors were produced by Georg Karl Urlaub in 1770, while those on the walls are by Christian Popp and Ernst Schwab. The walls of this room however suffered considerably through the fire in the Residence in 1945, and much of their decoration as well as the whole ceiling had to be reconstructed.

The remarkable inlaid floor, originally the work of the Bamberg court ébéniste Balthasar Hermann and now replaced, has a perplexing pattern created from dark and light exotic woods that produces a three-dimensional effect. The faience stove from Strassbourg, which has a vase-shaped upper section painted white with abundant gilding, is by Franz Paul Acker, 1766 (partially reconstructed). The various articles of furniture were painted to harmonize with the colours of the room.

Next double page: Green Lacquered Room of the Northern Imperial Apartments (Room 21)

Furnishings: 2 console tables, green with gold, carved with putti figures by Johann Peter Wagner, c. 1770 ■ 1 sofa and 2 armchairs in Louis Seize forms, green with gold, carved in 1774 by the Bamberg court ébéniste Balthasar Hermann ■ Gaming table with marquetry (walnut, mother-of-pearl, etc.) by the court cabinet-maker Franz Benedikt Schlecht, 1755–1757. On the table top the coat of arms of Prince-Bishop Adam Friedrich von Seinsheim of Würzburg ■ 8 sconces, two-armed, gilded bronze, in the Louis Seize style ■ Glass arm chandelier with coloured leaves and flowers, Johann Michael Faller, Würzburg, c. 1770, partially reconstructed.

22 SERVANTS' ROOM

Paintings (on loan from the Federal Republic of Germany): Hunting still life by Joannes Fyt (1611–1661) ■ Hunting and fruit still life by Frans Snyders (1579–1657).

Furnishings: 2 commodes, inlaid, German, c. 1790 ■ Basket chandelier, Dresden, c. 1809.

State Gallery

ROOMS 23 TO 29

Since 1974 an important branch gallery of the Bavarian State Painting Collections has been located in the so-called 'Rennweg Rooms' of the Residence. On the basis of the works produced by Tiepolo in Würzburg, the state gallery, which was reorganized in 2016, is dedicated to the great centuries of Venetian painting.

In addition to Titian and Tintoretto, Paolo Veronese was one of the most important artists in the golden age of painting in 16th-century Venice. In the gallery, two series of pictures produced in his atelier in particular illustrate the great tradition of the art and commercial metropolis. Works by Palma il Giovane and the Bassanos, who were the leading masters of the following generations of artists, document the continuation of this flourishing artistic period right into the 17th century. The devotional and history pictures, allegories and portraits on display give an insight into the social, political and religious life of the lagoon city. Two unusual pictures of events by Joseph Heintz the Younger depict Venice as a city of festivals and revelry.

The central feature of the presentation, in the former Theatre Hall of the Residence, is the juxtaposition of allegories of the virtues from Veronese's workshop and the altar painting created by Giovanni Domenico Tiepolo in 1754 for the abbey church of Münsterschwarzach. This shows how profoundly the work of the Late Baroque masters from Venice was influenced by the High Renaissance style of their city of origin. Tiepolo was celebrated by his contemporaries as the 'new Veronese'. At first glance, his painting conjures up the former splendour of Venice. Luca Carlevarijs's picture showing the reception of an ambassador however documents the extent to which the luxury-loving elite were in denial of the loss of their economic and political power.

The narrative scenes of Amigoni, Piazzetta, Pittoni and the two Tiepolos are depicted with intelligence and wit, plentiful use of light and strong colours. Their works in the second part of the gallery provide evidence of the Europe-wide dominance of Venetian painting in the 18th century. Unlike their predecessors, these masters only rarely produced paintings for the palaces and churches of their homeland. They successfully placed themselves at the service of the European princes and soon their elegant, decorative art was embellishing numerous residences north of the Alps.

CATALOGUE OF SELECTED WORKS

23 FIRST GALLERY ROOM

Leandro Bassano (1557–1622)
'Susanna and the two Elders', c. 1580–1590
Canvas, 115.9 x 145.6 cm
Inv. HuW 27

The story by the prophet Daniel of Susanna who while bathing is watched by two lustful old judges who blackmail and slander her, was created by Leandro Bassano from a picture by his father Jacopo. He transferred the scene into a verdant park landscape, a typical feature of late-16th-century paintings. While Susanna prepares herself for her bath with the help of her attendants, the two men in the background are already planning their villainous deed.

Paolo Veronese (successor), 'Sultan Orchard II', c. 1580

ORCANE II

24 SECOND GALLERY ROOM

Titian (c. 1485/90–1576), atelier or successors
'Mary Magdalene as a penitent', c. 1570–1590
Canvas, 125.5 x 93.4 cm
Inv. 5175

Titian painted the portrait of St Mary Magdalene as a beautiful penitent for important clients such as Philipp II and Cardinal Granvelle. Various versions of the lightly clad, repentant hermit by this master have been preserved. The numerous copies by his atelier and successors document the enduring interest in the motif. Mary Magdalene appears with her attributes – ointment jar, book and skull – in a rocky landscape and looks tearfully up to heaven. Titian presents the saint in the style of Venetian portraits of beauties: her physical attractions are more emphasized than concealed by her long hair, light garment and woven cloth.

Palma il Giovane (1544–1628)
'St Sebastian', c. 1610
Canvas, 141.8 x 112 cm
Inv. 575

Palma il Giovane became Venice's leading master in the generation of painters that succeeded Tintoretto and Veronese. Here, by contrast with his other comparable depictions of Sebastian's martyrdom, he focuses more on the motif of the monumental nude figure. Only the arrow that stands out prominently against the light sky is a reference to the martyrdom. Palma uses light and shade to create the powerful form of the saint's body, constrained in an artificial pose, and at the same time emphasizes his silhouette. What is particularly remarkable is that the head and upper body of the seated, bound saint lean so far forward that his face is hidden.

Paolo Veronese (1528–1588), atelier or circle
Fourteen portraits of Turkish sultans, c. 1580
Canvas, each c. 69 x 54 cm
Inv. 2236–2249

In the year 1578 the Venetian senate was informed by its envoy in Constantinople that the grand vizier wished to have portraits of the sultans by Venetian artists. One year later a series of portraits of all the sultans from the founding of the Ottoman Empire up to the then ruler

Murad III was delivered, most of which have now been lost. The portraits presented here were produced on the basis of the originals in the same atelier at around the same time. They were evidently the work of at least two artists who were familiar with Veronese's painting style. The series was originally intended to be presented chonologically, but read from right to left, with most of the portraits hung in twos so that the figures are presented in dialogue with one another. The current display takes this into account.

Leandro Bassano (1557–1622)
Portrait of the merchant Leonhard Hermann, c. 1575
Canvas, 133.4 x 95.5 cm
Inv. 8091

Leandro was a member of the dal Ponte artist family who were named after their home town of Bassano. He made a name for himself in Venice primarily as a portrait painter. The German merchant Leonhard Hermann worked in the lagoon city for several years and in 1571 held the office of consul at the Fondaco dei Tedeschi. Bassano shows him working on his correspondence dressed as befitted his position in a fur-trimmed coat (chamarre). A folded letter bears Hermann's address in Venice and confirms that the portrait was created between 1571 and 1582, during his stay in the city. On the table that is covered with a precious rug is an hour glass, serving as a reminder of earthly transience.

25 THIRD GALLERY ROOM

Luca Carlevarijs (1663–1730)
'Reception of the Venetian envoys at the Tower of London', after 1707
Canvas, 135.9 x 252 cm
Inv. 14560

The work of Carlevarijs marks the beginning of the golden age of veduta painting in 18th-century Venice. Diplomatic events were depicted against a background of artistically composed panoramic views. With this large-format painting, Carlevarijs documents the reception of the Venetian envoys Nicolò Erizzo and Alvise II Pisani by representatives of the English government. The elaborate reception ceremony takes place against the backdrop of the buildings of London. Small boats have just ferried the envoys to the banks of the Thames where magnificent coaches await them. As the painter had never been to London, he based his work on printed vedute.

26 FOURTH GALLERY ROOM

Antonio Bellucci (Venice 1654 – Venice 1726)
'Danae and Perseus on the Raft',
'Cupid and Psyche', c. 1710
Canvas, 123 x 176 cm and 111 x 170 cm
Inv. 914/915

For ten years Bellucci was the court painter of Elector Palatine Johann Wilhelm in Düsseldorf. He painted these two mythological pictures, which are to be understood as allegories of love, for the elector's gallery. Danaë, made pregnant by Zeus, is cast into the sea after the birth of her son Perseus by her father, Acrisios. Zeus protects them on their dangerous journey and guides them to the island of Seriphos. Here, the young Perseus is steering the raft through the billowing waves with a sail.

The beautiful king's daughter, Psyche, is not allowed to look at Cupid, who only comes to her at night. Her jealous sisters urge Psyche to murder her divine spouse on the grounds that he must be a monster. As Psyche approaches Cupid with a dagger and an oil lamp she is overwhelmed by his beauty. But Cupid is woken by a drop of hot oil and flies away.

Federico Bencovich (1677–1753)
'Hercules and Omphale', c. 1710–1715
Canvas, 130 x 108 cm
Inv. 11336

From 1715 Federico Bencovich, who had trained first in Venice and then for a longer period in Bologna, received important commissions from high-ranking German clerics. In the service of Lothar Franz von Schönborn, Prince-Bishop of Bamberg and Elector of Mainz, he produced work for Weissenstein Palace near Pommersfelden. In 1734 he was appointed court painter of Friedrich Carl von Schönborn, Prince-Bishop of Bamberg and Würzburg, and created various paintings for the Würzburg Residence and Court Chapel. The subject of this painting, taken from ancient mythology, had been popular since the Renaissance as an example of 'female power'. As a punishment for the murder of Iphitos, Hercules was sold to Omphale, the Queen of Lydia. Since even though he had to serve her as a slave he fell in love with her, the reversal of roles shown here – Hercules with a spindle and distaff and Omphale in a lion skin with a club – is laden with eroticism.

27 NORTHERN OVAL GALLERY HALL (FORMER OPERA THEATRE)

The initial plans for a princes' hall, for which François Cuvilliés the Elder had produced a wooden model in 1766, were never implemented. In this room that is now devoid of decoration there is nothing to indicate that the 21.50 x 15.80 m rotunda with a vault 9.70 m high reaching up into the upper mezzanine floor was built for Prince-Bishop Adam Friedrich von Seinsheim as an opera theatre, the 'pretty little theatre in Würzburg', as it was described by his brother. The theatre interior, with three semicircular rows of seats, a prince's box and a stage occupying almost all of the western half of the room, was however removed as early as 1790 under Prince-Bishop Ludwig von Erthal due to lack of use. First called the 'Old Library' (1820) it was finally renamed 'Carousel Hall' (1845) after a carousel originally acquired by Grand Duke Ferdinand III of Tuscany (r. 1806–1814) for the Werneck Summer Palace was set up here for the children of the Crown Prince and future King Ludwig I (This carousel is now part of the exhibition on the Tuscany period in Room 13c). Since 1931–1932 the Oval Hall has been used as a gallery hall.

Paolo Veronese (1528–1588), atelier
Four paintings with allegories of the virtues, c. 1580
Canvas, each around 207 x 133 cm

The four large-format canvas pictures form a complete cycle with the female personifications of the three theological virtues: Fides, Spes and Caritas (Faith, Hope and Charity) and the four cardinal virtues Justitia, Prudentia, Fortitudo and Temperantia (Justice, Prudence, Fortitude and Temperance). The motifs and the style indicate that they were produced by the Veronese atelier. The differences in quality are due to the fact that several of the master's fellow artists worked on the paintings.

'Fides and Spes'
Inv. 455

The enthroned figure of Fides (Faith) is characterized by the white robe and the chalice that refers to the sacrifice of the Mass. Spes (Hope), kneeling on the ground, is shown almost naked, departing from the usual tradition. Her folded hands and her depiction in combination with Fides, however, confirm the identity of this figure.

'Caritas'
Inv. 445

Of the four paintings, this depiction of Caritas (Charity) is closest in style and quality to Veronese's own work. Caritas

embodies the love of and for God and for others. In this composition, firmly established in the tradition of allegories, the female figure represents motherly love with her breast exposed and three children crowding around her playfully and seeking her protection.

'Justitia and Prudentia'
Inv. 447

Paolo Veronese (atelier), 'Justitia and Prudentia', c. 1580

With the sword and scales that are her attributes and represent judicial power and a balanced verdict, Justitia (Justice) is depicted standing in front of the tall base of a column on the left of the picture. Prudentia (Prudence) is sitting at her side looking in a mirror as a sign of critical self-awareness. As in the case of Spes (Hope), this allegorical figure is reminiscent of Venetian portraits of beauties, where the mirror is a symbol of vanity.

'Fortitudo and Temperantia'
Inv. 527

With her back to the viewer, Fortitudo (Fortitude) sits on the base of a broken ionic column that symbolizes her power. She is wearing blue armour and has her left foot on the capital of the fallen column on the ground. Temperantia (Temperance) proffers a golden cup and also holds a silver jug: she is adding water to the wine.

Joseph Heintz the Younger (c. 1600–1678)
'Il Ridotto' (The Gaming Room in the Palazzo Dandolo), c. 1648
Canvas, 136 x 163 cm
Inv. 2621

Joseph Heintz the Younger, who came from Augsburg, lived and worked in Venice from 1625 onwards. He was mainly interested in capturing social occasions, state ceremonies and folk festivals in the city on the lagoon. These works are largely exaggerated renderings of events, painted in a very cursory style. With this unusual view of the interior of the palazzo, the painter shows the gaming room opened by Marco Dandolo in 1638, which was made famous by the memoires of Casanova.

Joseph Heintz the Younger (c. 1600–1678)
'Contest on the Ponte dei Pugni', c. 1648
Canvas, 135 x 192 cm
Inv. 3657

Ever since the 14th century, groups from rival districts in Venice had been traditionally holding boxing matches on the Ponte dei Pugni (Bridge of Fists). This violent spectacle, to which Heintz gives a bizarre slant, was prohibited in 1705. The artist repeatedly painted this motif, which was also popular amongst visitors to the city. Despite their careless execution, his extremely lively views of Venice are important forerunners of the 18th century vedute.

Giovanni Domenico Tiepolo (1727 – 1804)
'The Stoning of St Stephen', 1754
Canvas, 390.5 x 204.5 cm
Inv. 15687

This highly dramatic depiction of St Stephen's martyrdom is a major work by the young artist, who had previously assisted his father with the painting of the frescoes in the Residence. There is a tense contrast between the saint and his murderers: while the tormentors, painted in dark colours, are about to hurl huge rocks at him, Stephen, who is bathed in bright light, gazes ecstatically up to heaven. As he faces death the Holy Trinity and an angel with a crown and palm frond appear to him. The abbot of the Benedictine monastery of Münsterschwarzach commissioned the painting for a side altar of the abbey church that was pulled down in the 19th century.

Giovanni Domenico Tiepolo, 'The Stoning of St Stephen', 1754

Jacopo Amigoni,
'Venus and
Adonis', c. 1740

28 FIFTH GALLERY ROOM

Giovanni Domenico Tiepolo (1727–1804)
'Christ and Mary Magdalene in the home of
Simon the Pharisee',
'The Last Supper', 1752
Canvas, each 99.2 x 150 cm
Inv. 1162/1163

While assisting his father with the frescoes in the Residence, Giovanni Domenico also worked on his own account in Würzburg and painted several pictures on canvas. In these works he clearly expresses his own style. The two scenes from the New Testament represent the sacraments of the Confession and the Eucharist.

'The Last Supper' is dominated by the ecstatic emotion of the apostles. The apostle on the left with the white hair and beard, in an attitude of humility, is Peter, Christ's first disciple who denied him three times. The bible story is presented as a timeless event with a clear reference to the transubstantiation at Communion. The establishment of the Eucharist is thus the topic of the picture, and its counterpart, showing the encounter of Christ and Magdalene, describes the sacrament of Confession. A weeping sinner, traditionally equated with Mary Magdalene, kneels in front of Jesus at a feast, dries his feet with her hair and anoints them as a sign of her repentance.

29 SIXTH GALLERY ROOM

Giovanni Battista Pittoni (1687–1767)
'The Magnanimity of Scipio',
'The Sacrifice of Polyxena', c. 1735–1740
Canvas, each 134 x 160 cm
Inv. HuW 32/HuW 33

With Scipio's noble deed and 'The Sacrifice of Polyxena' as its counterpart, Pittoni chose two contrasting classical themes of history painting and created compositions in the theatrical, decorative Venetian Rococo style. According to Livy, the general Scipio Africanus was given a beautiful virgin as war booty after he had taken New Carthage. However, when he heard that she was engaged to be married he returned her to her bridegroom, Allucius. He also gave her the treasures that her parents had offered him for her freedom.

The story of Polyxena, the daughter of the Trojan king Priamos, is related in Ovid's *Metamorphoses*. In Pittoni's light-filled dramatization, however, there is little trace of the barbarity of her fate. At the centre of the picture Neoptolemos, Achilles' son, orders Polyxena's sacrificial death. She is already kneeling at an altar in front of his father's tomb. Achilles, who was mortally wounded by Paris, had demanded the sacrifice of Polyxena if Troy should fall.

Jacopo Amigoni (1682–1752)
'Venus and Adonis', c. 1740
Canvas 144.2 x 173.5 cm
Inv. 2857

Amigoni's career took him all over Europe – in Munich he received commissions from the elector and he ultimately became court painter in Madrid. This painting from the collection of the Elector of Cologne is a characteristic example of his charming, light and cheerful style. Surrounded by amoretti, Venus sleeps in a beguiling pose in a glade. Venus had to share her lover, the hunter Adonis, with the goddess of the underworld, so that he was only ever at her side for half the year. The picture shows his annual arrival in spring with the heralds of the season, the wind god Zephyr and the nymph Chloris, embracing on a cloud.

Giovanni Battista Tiepolo (1696–1770)
'Rinaldo under the Spell of Armida'
'Rinaldo's parting from Armida', c. 1752–1753
Canvas, each 105 x 40 cm
Inv. ResMü.G0840/ResMü.G0841
(On loan from the Bavarian Palace Administration, Munich)

While working on the frescoes in the Würzburg Residence, Tiepolo also completed several paintings on canvas – including these two, originally owned by the prince-bishop, that show scenes from Torquato Tasso's *Gerusalemme liberata*. The heroic epic relates the story of the Christian knight Rinaldo who has set out to liberate Jerusalem but is enticed by the heathen sorceress Armida. He succumbs to her charms in an Arcadian garden while his comrades – seen in the background of the picture – approach to rescue him.

'Rinaldo under the Spell of Armida', painting by G. B. Tiepolo, Würzburg, 1753

The masterful narrative skill and lightness typical of Tiepolo's painting is similarly reflected in the counterpart to the lovers' idyll. The artist transforms the park-like surroundings into a landscape of ruins for the parting scene. In this setting, the brightly illuminated figures, in costumes of strong, harmonious colours, are presented at the moment the magic spell loses its power. Rinaldo's comrades beseech him urgently, in spite of his longing, to take leave of Armida, who is shown lamenting on the ground.

Ingelheim Rooms

(First Episcopal Apartment; Seinsheim Rooms)

ROOMS 30 TO 39

The so-called First Episcopal Apartment, located as
planned under Johann Philipp Franz von Schönborn (r.
1719–1724) here in the north block that was the first section of the Residence to be built, was furnished under his
successor Christoph Franz von Hutten (r. 1725–1729) although not quite completed before he died. The walls
were decorated with tapestries and large landscape paintings, which Franz Ignaz Roth painted in 1727 'in oils [di-
rectly] on the walls'. All that has remained from this first
decoration phase is a fireplace (Room 37) and the stucco-
work of the ceiling coves in seven rooms, created in the
Régence style by Johann Peter and Karl Anton Castelli
in 1724–1725. Begun immediately after Balthasar Neumann's trip to Paris, this is the oldest stucco-work in the
Residence.

Friedrich Carl von Schönborn (r. 1729–1746) also used
these rooms until 1737, when he was able to move into the
so-called Second Episcopal Apartment in the cour d'honneur and city wing of the south block (the subsequent Tuscany Rooms and present art gallery of the Martin von
Wagner Museum). All the following prince-bishops also
lived there, with the exception of Schönborn's immediate
successor Anselm Franz von Ingelheim (r. 1746–1749),
who preferred the First Episcopal Apartment. Although it
was this occupant who gave the rooms their name, it was
not until 30 years later, under Adam Friedrich von Seinsheim (r. 1755–1779), that the important, second phase of
decoration began.

*Hall of the Ingel-
heim Rooms with
the portrait of
Friedrich Carl
von Schönborn
(Room 31)*

The decoration of the Ingelheim Rooms completed in 1776–1781, the last major project of the 18th century, marked the end of the external and internal work on the Residence, which had continued without interruption for almost 60 years. As the independent achievement of the court stucco-worker Materno Bossi – in cooperation with the court sculptor Peter Wagner (furniture) – they are the stylistic highpoint of the Seinsheim era. After the fire in 1945, the partially destroyed ceilings and floors were reconstructed, the damaged walls were restored and completed and in 1978 the whole apartment was reopened together with its furniture, most of which had been saved and similarly been restored.

Following the work on the halls in the north block (Opera Theatre in the Northern Oval, Princes' Hall), in 1776 Prince-Bishop Adam Friedrich v. Seinsheim commissioned the court stucco-worker Materno Bossi to redecorate the Ingelheim Rooms in the form in which they appear today. In addition to the state rooms on the garden side, the upgraded, modernized rooms provided, 'another place for holding dinners and social gatherings', as was stated on the occasion of their first use in 1778. They also functioned as a guest apartment, as revealed by the description of the rooms in the inventory of 1778: on either side of the central hall were an antechamber, bedroom, cabinet and valet's room.

The colourful appearance of the Early Neoclassical decoration – silvered stucco on coloured wall surfaces – was the result of Seinsheim's connections with Munich (Munich Residence, Amalienburg and Schleißheim New Palace). In 1776 the stucco-worker visited Munich to study the work there. The use of stucco as the sole decoration material follows the general trend already evident in the northern state rooms; the sopraportas are decorated not with paintings but with stucco reliefs of outstanding quality by Materno Bossi. As in the gardens of the Seinsheim era, the reliefs are dominated by putti.

For the individual stucco decorations, Materno Bossi partially incorporated the stucco ceilings of the first phase of decoration and used them as his source of inspiration, as shown clearly, for example, by Room 33, which continues the theme of music and Room 36 with its floral motifs. He even took ideas for the representations of the continents in the hall (Room 31) from G. B. Tiepolo's staircase fresco, and in fact the entire content of the hall decoration reflects the fresco programme of the staircase.

However, the Würzburg stucco-worker also drew on French engravings in the Louis Seize style that was in fashion at the time; this gives the Ingelheim Rooms their characteristic appearance and distinguishes them both from the decorations at the end of the Rococo era and the brief phase of early goût grec in the northern state rooms. Bossi used the *Nouvelle Iconologie Historique* of Jean Charles Delafosse, which was published in Paris in 1771. The decoration ideas this contains are intended to express symbolic meanings and are highly individual (Fig: p. 147). Even though Bossi used and adapted these models without regard to their meaning, they have retained some of the distinctive Delafosse characteristics. The furniture of the Ingelheim Rooms, such as the stoves supplied from Vienna and some of the painted furniture made by the court sculptor Peter Wagner is also influenced by Delafosse's models.

The Ingelheim Rooms are thus the main example of a version of the Delafosse style in a Main-Franconian interpretation, which replaced the goût grec in the Residence as a short-lived variation of the Zopfstil (Late Rococo). For the last time, the room decoration and appointments were not only conceived as a synthesis of the arts, but were also influenced by the previous epochs of decoration that had succeeded one another since the Residence was begun.

30 SERVANTS' ROOM ADJOINING THE INGELHEIM ROOMS

In the cavetto of this room, which is otherwise devoid of decoration, is the stucco-work with Régence motifs that was created in 1724–1725 by Johann Peter Castelli for the First Episcopalian Apartment.

Painting 'Summer landscape' by F. H. Paradyen, 1749, Zerbst Palace ▪ Commode, with three drawers, cherrywood, German, c. 1790.

31 HALL OF THE INGELHEIM ROOMS

Engraved model for the stucco-work of the window piers in the Hall of the Ingelheim Rooms. From the Nouvelle Iconologie Historique of J. Ch. Delafosse, Paris, 1771

The Hall occupies the middle three window axes and the entire depth of the town wing of the north block. The flat ceiling, which is 50 cm higher than that of the other rooms, and the windows on both sides give it the character of a hall. The decoration on the walls and ceilings, which is all from the second phase of work on the interior and consists entirely of stucco-work, was created by the court stucco-worker Materno Bossi in 1776–1778 based on the engraved designs of the French architect Jean Charles Delafosse. In 1778 the room was still known as the 'New Red Hall' and was probably painted entirely in white in the early 19th century. After the war damage of 1945, restoration of the interior shell of the Hall and the adjoining apartments was completed in 1978.

The stucco decoration celebrates the person and reign of Prince-Bishop Adam Friedrich v. Seinsheim who commissioned the work: above the stove in the middle of the end wall is his coat of arms, and on the opposite wall his likeness as a relief medallion, both flanked by two Caesarean busts as a symbol of glorious apotheosis. The actual message is contained in the middle ceiling section, where a customary image is used equating the prince with the sun;

as the 'sun of the country' he spreads the benefit of his rule over all the land and people like the light and warmth of the sun. Under his rule, trade flourishes and the arts prosper. This is represented by the initials AF in the sun on the ceiling, by the four continents above the mirrors, by the depictions of science and commerce, architecture, sculpture and painting in the reliefs above the doors, by the musical instruments on the ceiling and by the relief busts, which probably represent female singers and musicians. The programme thus clearly follows that of the staircase fresco by G. B. Tiepolo, and the stucco-worker also referred to it with his successful rendering of the four continents as puttos.

With the state portrait of the Prince-Bishop Friedrich Carl v. Schönborn (r. 1729–1746) set into the southern end wall, Seinsheim honours his great model and also refers to the fact that his uncle had been the first to live in the Ingelheim Rooms, if only briefly as a provisional measure, 40 years before.

Painting: State portrait of Prince-Bishop Friedrich Carl von Schönborn (r. 1729–1746), full length, pointing to Schönborn Palace near Göllersdorf (repetition of the portrait in the Princes' Hall).

147

Furnishings: 2 x 2 console tables, Joh. P. Wagner, 1776–1780, painted white and silvered. Two of the tables already bear the initials of Prince-Bishop Franz Ludwig von Erthal ■ 4 bronze statuettes on Boulle plinths, allegories of the four elements, Paris, c. 1725 ■ 24 sconces (8 five-armed, 16 three-armed) with metal foliage, originally from a design by Materno Bossi (reconstructed) ■ 8 sconces on either side of the mirrors, three-armed, probably originally from a design by M. Bossi, cast brass (reconstructed) ■ 2 glass arm chandeliers with pendeloques ■ Large faience stove, glazed white, probably designed by M. Bossi, 1776–1777, supplied from Vienna (partially reconstructed).

32 RED ANTECHAMBER OF THE INGELHEIM ROOMS (HUNTING ROOM)

The silvered stucco decorations on a pale red ground were completed in two phases around 50 years apart. The stucco-work of the cavetto, including the corner cartouches, was designed by the stucco-worker Johann Peter Castelli to the specifications of the Paris architect German Boffrand and produced 'from the drawing of the hunt' in 1724–1725 for the First Episcopal Apartment. The stucco-work on the walls and the ceiling rosette, however, is Zopfstil ornamentation created in 1776–1778 during the Seinsheim era by the court stucco-worker Materno Bossi, who based his work on the engraved designs of Jean Charles Delafosse; the motif above the mirror, for example, is taken from the model entitled 'Abissinie ou haute Ethiopie et la Religion'. The hunting theme which gave the room its name also featured in the second decoration phase, as shown by Bossi's sopraporta reliefs with three hunting scenes. They depict fishing, the hunting of game birds and the hunting of hares using hawks.

Furnishings: Console table, G. A. Guthmann, c. 1740, painted pale red and silvered ■ 6 upholstered chairs, Joh. P. Wagner,

1778–1780, painted pale red and silvered, silk damask covering matching the colour of the wall coverings (replaced) ■ Commode with two drawers, Franconian, c. 1785. Veneered with walnut and walnut root wood ■ Writing cabinet belonging to Prince-Bishop Franz Ludwig von Erthal, Main-Franconian, c. 1780. Veneered and inlaid with walnut, walnut root wood, mahogany, rosewood and palisander, gilded bronze fittings. The front of the upper section can be folded down for use as a writing surface and the middle pilaster with the initials FL functions as the support. The upper section can be closed inside with a partition that operates like a roller blind. The lower section has doors at the side and drawers behind them. The counterpart of this writing cabinet belonging to the prince-bishop's brother, the Mainz elector Friedrich Carl von Erthal, is in Aschaffenburg Palace ■ Ivory sculpture 'The Sacrifice of Isaac' by Simon Troger, Munich, c. 1760 ■ Bronze statuette of Diana by court sculptor Claude Curé, Würzburg, 1724. Plinth signed: 'Claud Curé scul: J:A: Roth fud: 1724' ■ 2 sconces, three-armed, probably originally from a design by M. Bossi, cast bronze (reconstructed) ■ Glass arm chandelier with pendeloques ■ Faience stove, glazed white, Vienna, 1776–1777 (partially reconstructed).

33 GREEN WRITING ROOM OF THE INGELHEIM ROOMS (MUSIC ROOM)

In this room too, the stucco-work begun under Prince-Bishop Johann Philipp Franz von Schönborn in the first decoration phase of the Residence is combined with that of the Seinsheim era: Johann Peter Castelli produced the stucco-work of the ceiling and cavetto in the Régence style in 1724–1725, which he designed to the specifications of Germain Boffrand. The theme of the decorations is music, with representations of various instruments, so that this was also known as the Music Room. Over 50 years later, in 1776 to 1778, Materno Bossi created the Zopfstil decoration of the walls, dominated by the motif of the bucranium (steer skull) with the laurel wreath above a rosette frieze; for his work here he used 'Siam et la Religion' from the *Nouvelle Iconologie Historique* of Jean Charles Delafosse. The theme of the Régence decoration was taken up again by Bossi, not in the sopraporta reliefs, which depict bowls of fruit, but in the window niches with the hanging arrangements of musical instruments.

Tapestries: 3 tapestries from the 'Fins Teniers' series with depictions of rural life based on motifs by David Teniers. Entrance wall: Skaters and hog slaughtering, Brussels, Jerome de Clerc, c. 1710. Rear wall: The fish catch, Brussels, signed 'A.CASTRO' (= Jasper van der Borght), c. 1710. Exit wall: Archery, Lille (?), c. 1720–1730.

Furnishings: Suite of seating furniture, consisting of 2 upholstered chairs, 4 armchairs (bergères) and a two-seat sofa, Joh. P. Wagner, 1778/80. Painted pale green and silvered to match the room, coverings in greenish silk damask (replaced) ▪ Console table, G. A. Guthmann, c. 1740, painted green and silvered ▪ 2 commodes with two drawers, Main-Franconian, c. 1780, veneered in birch burl and walnut, inlaid oval medallion with musical instruments on the front ▪ 2 alabaster groups of fighting gladiators by Joh. W. van der Auwera, Würzburg, 1738. The group with the net-fighter is signed on the plinth: 'I. WOL: V. AUWERA. F: 1738' ▪ 2 sconces, three-armed, probably originally from a design by M. Bossi, cast brass (reconstructed) ▪ Glass arm chandelier by Johann Michael Faller, Würzburg, c. 1770 (partially reconstructed) ▪ Faience stove, glazed white, Vienna, 1776–1777 (partially reconstructed).

34 YELLOW CORNER CABINET OF THE INGELHEIM ROOMS

The corner room facing the Rennweg and the Rosenbachhof with its silvered stucco-work on a yellow ground also reflects the two different phases of decoration in the

Régence style and Zopfstil. On the ceiling and in the cavetto are the decorations created in 1724–1725 by Johann Peter Castelli for the First Episcopal Apartment, whereas the stucco-work of the walls by Materno Bossi was not completed until 1776–1778. The fireplace decorations and the elaborate pattern of the floor, which is inlaid with different-coloured woods (reconstructed), are both based on engravings from the *Recueil d'Architecture* by the French architect Jean François de Neufforge. The fireplace itself (reconstructed) is a later addition from the Tuscany period (1806–1814). The decoration with floral bouquets in the ceiling stucco-work, a basket with produce from the sea as a sopraporta relief and stucco musical instruments hanging above the door to the adjoining room has no uniform theme.

Painting (on loan from the Bavarian State Painting Collections): Portrait of Prince-Bishop Adam Friedrich v. Seinsheim, Joh. Jos. Scheubel the Younger, 1766.

Furnishings: 6 upholstered chairs, Joh. P. Wagner, 1778–1780, painted yellow and silvered to match the colour scheme of the room, the golden yellow silk damask coverings – as well as the wall covering – have been replaced ▪ Commode with three drawers and rounded corners, on six legs, Southern German, c. 1785 ▪ Dressing table, inlaid with floral marquetry, by Franz Benedikt Schlecht or Johann Georg Fellwöck, Würzburg, c. 1770 ▪ Marble group 'Pluto abducting Proserpina', possibly by Joh. W. van der Auwera, Würzburg, c. 1740 ▪ Glass arm chandelier (copy, cf. Room 33).

35 BLUE ANTECHAMBER OF THE INGELHEIM ROOMS

Apart from the Hall, the Blue Antechamber is the only room in the suite where everything, including the ceiling stucco-work, was replaced when the rooms were redecorated during the Seinsheim era in 1776–1778. The stucco-worker Materno Bossi based the motifs of the silvered stucco wall decoration on a pale blue-green ground on a design from the *Nouvelle Iconologie Historique* of Jean Charles Delafosse entitled 'Irlande et sa Religion'. In the cavettos are martial trophies, which also feature in the decorations in the window jambs, together with animal attributes alluding to the four continents portrayed in Tiepolo's staircase fresco. The putti in the five reliefs above the three doors, the stove niche and the mirror are by contrast quite unwarlike: they are shown waiting on Diana, goddess of the hunt, and thus represent the theme of hunting and fishing.

Blue Antechamber of the Ingelheim Rooms (Room 35)

Furnishings: Suite of seating furniture, consisting of 8 armchairs and a sofa together with 2 console tables and 1 table, Joh. P. Wagner, 1776–1779. Painted pale blue-green and silvered to match the colour scheme of the room; the silk damask coverings of the chairs have been replaced to match the wall covering. The tables were based on a model from the *Nouvelle Iconologie Historique* of J. Ch. Delafosse entitled 'la Perse' ■ Bronze statuette 'Jupiter and eagle' from an ancient model, Italian, 17th century ■ 2 sconces, three-armed, cast brass (reconstructed) ■ Glass arm chandelier by Johann Michael Faller, Würzburg, c. 1770 (partially reconstructed) ■ Faience stove, glazed white, Vienna, 1776–1777 (partially reconstructed).

36 YELLOW AUDIENCE ROOM OF THE INGELHEIM ROOMS

The stucco decoration of the room again combines the two decoration phases, that of the Régence period under the founder of the Residence, Prince-Bishop Johann Philipp Franz von Schönborn, and that of the Zopfstil era under Prince-Bishop Adam Friedrich von Seinsheim in the 18th century. The stucco-work of the ceiling and the

cavetto with the motifs of the ruler's insignias, fruit and flowers were designed by the stucco-worker Johann Peter Castelli to the specifications of the architect Germain Boffrand and produced in 1724–1725. It was not until over 50 years later that the wall decoration was added by the court stucco-worker Materno Bossi, who took up the floral motifs of the existing stucco-work: the sopraporta reliefs are wreathed with roses, and show putti playing with garlands, above the stove is a flower basket and in the stucco drapery in the window jambs, representations of the four seasons. Here too, Materno Bossi used two illustrations from the *Nouvelle Iconologie Historique* of Jean Charles Delafosse entitled 'Moscovie' and 'Contrariété'.

Tapestries: 3 tapestries from the 'Fins Teniers' series with depictions of rural life from motifs by David Teniers. Entrance wall: Peasants at skittles, Brussels, Jerome de Clerc, c. 1710. Rear wall: Country fair, Brussels, de Clerc, c. 1710. Exit wall: Pastoral scene, Brussels, signed 'A.CASTRO' (= Jasper van der Borght), c. 1710.

Furnishings: 6 armchairs, Joh. P. Wagner, 1776–1780, painted yellow and silvered to match the colour scheme of the room, yellow silk damask coverings (replaced) ■ Console table, Joh. P. Wagner, 1772–1774, painted yellow and silvered ■ 2 commodes, Franconian, c. 1785, veneered in walnut and with various inlays, fittings with porcelain knobs ■ Writing desk with a semicircular closure (bureau à cylindre), Franconian, c. 1780, veneered with walnut, cherrywood and mahogany, inlaid work in a perspective pattern ■ Bust 'Truth', green-and-white marble with bronze, Pierre François Le Jeune, Stuttgart, c. 1776 (signed: 'LE JEUNE') ■ 2 sconces, three-armed, cast brass (reconstructed) ■ Glass arm chandelier (copy, cf. Room 33) ■ Faience stove, glazed white, Vienna, 1776–1777 (partially reconstructed).

37 GREEN CORNER CABINET OF THE INGELHEIM ROOMS

In addition to the stucco-work on the ceiling, for which the stucco-worker Johann Peter Castelli was paid in 1725, this room also contains the grey marble fireplace built by the sculptor Peter Heiliger for the First Episcopal Apartment, which is the oldest fireplace in the Residence. It bears the coat of arms of Prince-Bishop Christoph Franz von Hutten (r. 1725–1729). Materno Bossi based the wall decoration of the Seinsheim era, originating in 1776–1778, on an engraving from Jean Charles Delafosse's *Nouvelle Iconologie Historique* entitled 'Abissinie ou haute Ethiopie et la Religion'. This is the theme of the decoration around the window opening onto the cour d'honneur in the axis of the suite. Antique-style bust medallions, fruit baskets and putti playing and making music are the dominant features of the decoration.

Furnishings: 3 armchairs, Joh. P. Wagner, 1776–1780, painted green and silvered to match the colour scheme of the room, silk damask coverings (replaced) ▪ Console table, Joh. P. Wagner, 1772–1774, painted green and silvered to match the colour scheme of the room ▪ Fire screen, c. 1780, painted green and silvered, with green silk damask covering ▪ Lady's roll-top bureau, Franconian, c. 1770, oak veneered with exotic woods, inlaid with a chequered pattern ▪ Wall clock, wood, carved and gilded, probably Franconian, c. 1780 ▪ Marble group 'Nessus and Deianeira', 18th century ▪ 2 sconces, three-armed, cast brass (reconstructed) ▪ Crystal chandelier, Vienna, c. 1750 ▪ 2 simple andirons and set of 3 fire irons, 18th century.

38 HUTTEN CABINET (NOT ACCESSIBLE)

The ceiling stucco-work is by Johann Peter Castelli, 1725, with allegories of the virtues in the corners: Justice, Truth, Temperance and Fortitude. In the lambrequins under these figures are the coat of arms and the initials of Prince-Bishop Christoph Franz von Hutten (r. 1725–1729). The stucco reliefs of hunting spoils (game birds) above the stove niche and over the door were created in 1776–1778 by Materno Bossi.

39 SERVANTS' ROOM ADJOINING THE INGELHEIM ROOMS

Painting 'Winter landscape' by F. H. Paradyen, c. 1749, from Zerbst Palace ▪ Commode with three doors, cherrywood, German, c. 1790.

40 CHARLOTTE CORRIDOR

In the prince bishops' era, there were servants' rooms here. The Corridor is named after Princess Charlotte Auguste Karoline, daughter of the Bavarian king Max I Joseph, whose second marriage in 1816 was to Emperor Franz I of Austria, who had been widowed three times. Before her wedding she lived here in 1815–1816 in a suite of rooms facing the cour d'honneur (destroyed in 1945). This suite was originally furnished for his daughters by Grand Duke Ferdinand III of Tuscany, brother of the emperor, who ruled in Würzburg in 1806–1814.

41 ANTECHAMBER TO THE PRINCES' HALL

Paintings: King Max I Joseph of Bavaria (r. 1806–1825), depicted here while still elector (r. 1799–1805), before the elevation of Bavaria to a kingdom, c. 1800–1805 ▪ King Ludwig I of Bavaria (r. 1825–1848), anonymous copy after Joseph Stieler, after 1826 ▪ King Maximilian II of Bavaria (r. 1848–1864), c. 1850 ▪ King Ludwig II of Bavaria (r. 1864–1886), August Spiess, c. 1875 ▪ Prince Regent Luitpold of Bavaria (r. 1886–1912), August Holmberg, 1898.

Furnishing: Large iron stove with the coat of arms of Prince-Bishop Friedrich Carl von Schönborn.

Princes' Hall (Princes' Gallery)

Although it is located in the transverse wing constructed from 1726 to 1728 between the two inner courtyards of the north block, the Princes' Hall was only completed in 1772 under Prince-Bishop Adam Friedrich von Seinsheim (r. 1755–1779). The original plan (1723) to site the Court Chapel here was abandoned and the furnishing of the hall as a music room in 1766–1770 was only provisional. The court used it as a dining room or a room for games and gathered here before the opera performances in the adjacent Northern Oval. The room decoration was severely damaged in 1945 and completely destroyed above the entablature; the restoration, incorporating the original oil paintings, was completed in 1978.

The oblong room, one-and-a-half storeys high with windows on both sides, extends over five window axes. There are two deep music galleries at either end, under each of which is a fireplace with a mirror between two doors. Above a wainscot of grey marble the walls are decorated with white stucco lustro, with pilasters in the Corinthian style. These support a very high entablature area, which hides the original higher and round-arched outline of the windows (still visible from outside), designed when the room was to have been the chapel. Below the flat ceiling is a continuous cavetto with 24 (reconstructed) stucco reliefs by Materno Bossi: putti engaged in seasonal activities alternate with putti with vases. A bishop's portrait is inset into each of the eight window piers between two pilasters, crowned with a stucco relief showing trophies and the ap-

State portrait of the last ruler to influence the design of the Residence in the 18th century, Prince-Bishop Adam Friedrich von Seinsheim (r. 1755–1779), by G. Desmarées, 1763–1764 (Room 42)

159

propriate coat of arms. The gallery balustrade is also decorated with the coat of arms and initials of Seinsheim. Built into the false fireplaces made of yellow stucco marble are iron stoves with wrought iron rosette grilles above them on either side from the workshop of Georg Oegg.

The court architects Johann Philipp Geigel and Johann Michael Fischer were responsible for the structural planning, and in 1771–1772 the court stucco-worker Materno Bossi created the stucco decoration. Like the staircase, the room is in the goût grec style, a variation of Neoclassicism originating from France, which was popular at the time. The decoration scheme, planned long beforehand in 1765, was Prince-Bishop Adam Friedrich v. Seinsheim's own idea. At a time when the justification and continuation of the ecclesiastical principalities was being increasingly questioned, the eight full-length state portraits of Würzburg prince-bishops – of Seinsheim himself, and his seven immediate predecessors – were intended to emphasize the well-established sovereign tradition as well as the sovereign claim of the Würzburg prince-bishops. In 1764 and 1765, the painter at the Bavarian electoral court, Georg Desmarées, delivered two state portraits of Seinsheim: the full-figure one was installed here and the smaller half-length portrait was hung in a room with a similar purpose in Seinsheim's second bishop's seat, the New Residence of Bamberg. The Princes' Hall is therefore to be interpreted as a memorial to the ecclesiastical principality of Würzburg.

Portraits (set in the walls) of the eight prince-bishops:
Joh. Gottfried von Guttenberg (r. 1684–1698)
Joh. Philipp von Greiffenclau (r. 1699–1719), painted in 1719
Joh. Philipp Franz von Schönborn (r. 1719–1724) attributed to J. P. Feuerlein
Christoph Franz von Hutten (r. 1724–1729) by Jo. Ad. Remela (signed)

Friedrich Carl von Schönborn (r. 1729–1746)
Anselm Franz von Ingelheim (r. 1746–1749)
Carl Philipp von Greiffenclau (r. 1749–1754)
Adam Friedrich von Seinsheim (r. 1755–1779) by
Georg Desmarées, 1763–1764.

Furnishings: 2 chandeliers (new) from models from the
Albertina, Vienna.

*Prince-Bishop
Friedrich Carl
von Schönborn,
full-figure state
portrait*

161

Court Chapel

Court Chapel, looking towards the altar

The shell of the Court Chapel in the Würzburg Residence was built under Prince-Bishop Friedrich Carl von Schönborn (r. 1729–1746) in 1732–1733. Its architect, who was also responsible for the whole of the Residence, was Balthasar Neumann, who coordinated the staff of artists and craftsmen working on the interior of the chapel. When most of the elaborate decoration was finished, the chapel was consecrated to the Holy Trinity on 15 September 1743.

Planning and location

The only feature of the Court Chapel in the south-west corner of the Würzburg Residence that is visible from outside is the relatively small portal, with a few steps leading up to it and modest sculptural decoration. And there is no tower; the indispensible church bells are almost hidden away in a roof turret on the transverse wing between the two inner courtyards of the south block. The two outside walls of the chapel, the three-axis entrance façade facing the Residenzplatz and the long side facing the Court Garden with eight window axes that extends as far as the Southern Oval, have the same four-storey façade system as the rest of the Residence.

The various architects involved in the planning of the building complex that was begun in 1720 each envisaged a different location for the Court Chapel, but initially it was always going to be in the north block. Balthasar Neumann planned it first as a simple rectangular room in the

the diagonally opposite north-east corner, Maximilian von Welsch then sited it as a central room in the Oval in the middle of the north side, Robert de Cotte put it in the centre of the building where the Staircase Hall is now located, opposite another staircase hall on the south side, and Germain Boffrand put it back in the Northern Oval, extended by a choir in the transverse wing between the courtyards of the north block. This plan is visible from the original round-arched windows that were actually completed and can still be seen from outside on the main floor of this transverse wing (today the Princes' Hall). The construction of the whole Northern Oval was however then stopped and the Court Chapel was finally built in the south-west corner of the Residence from new plans drawn up by Balthasar Neumann in the year 1732.

Altar with altar painting 'The Assumption of Mary', by G. B. Tiepolo, 1752

Interior design

It comes as a surprise to every visitor that the absolutely straight external walls of the Court Chapel conceal an interior consisting entirely of curving walls. With its complicated architectonic design, compounded by the elaborate architectural and sculptural ornamentation, it is not immediately obvious how the chapel is structured, even though the relatively small room can almost all be seen only a few steps in from the door (interior length 34.95 m, width 13.35 m, height 18.75 m). In the ground plan and in the vault, Balthasar Neumann inserted into what was actually a rectangular space three adjoining ovals one behind the other, two small, transverse oval rotundas above the entrance and the choir area, which flank a large, longitudinal oval where the two side altars are located. This structure is most clearly visible in the vault, where the two smaller oval domes above the music gallery and the main altar frame the larger central dome. The domes open out towards each other so that the vertexes of their wide arches touch. The spandrels between the oval rotundas are en-

closed by concavely curving wall areas, each of which surrounds a window axis, and triangular vaulting caps.

The interior of the chapel is dominated by the prominent division of the walls into two sections by the wide horizontal band of the stucco-marble entablature zone, which is supported by 22 smooth stucco marble columns with gilded composite capitals. 16 of these columns stand immediately in front of the wall pilasters or merge with them as three-quarter columns. Over the main cornice, short pilasters, which continue these columns upwards, support the base of the dome vault. The pilasters, richly decorated with gold ornamentation, are in turn divided into two sections and only the lower half is fluted. The other columns standing freely in the room support the music gallery in the entrance bay and the altar gallery in the choir bay. The front of the two balconies swings out from the wall into the room following the line of the large entablature. While the alternating concave-convex-concave altar gallery with its smaller radius fits into the choir oval, the entirely concave curve of the music gallery continues the curve of the adjoining spandrel bay to form a semi-oval, thus creating a secondary shape contrary to that of the ground plan and vault. The two oratories on either side of the altar gallery are a further contrasting feature. They are located in the concave spandrel bays, but project convexly together with part of the supporting entablature into the room. The outstanding carvings of these wooden oratories are by Johann Adam Guthmann.

The original designs for the side altars are the work of Lucas von Hildebrandt, the architect at the imperial court in Vienna; as he was greatly admired by Prince-Bishop Friedrich Carl von Schönborn, Neumann was obliged to integrate some of his plans and suggestions. From their sheer size alone, but also because of their architectonic design, they look less like additional furnishing than integral elements of the architecture. With their black and yellow marble, turned, agate-coloured marble columns and abundant sculptural decoration, they are prominent features of the interior, and the two large altar paintings by Giovanni Battista Tiepolo are undoubtedly the most important works of art in the chapel.

The structure of the walls is so skilful that it is easy to overlook the fact that the zone below the main cornice is lit by the usual ground-floor and mezzanine windows, and the zone above by the usual main floor windows of the Residence façade. The lunette caps of the upper floor windows extend far into the dome vault, so that the windows of the upper mezzanine floor above it are no longer visible from inside, but are already in the attic floor outside the domes. From the straight lintels of the windows (only the mezzanine windows are enclosed by segmental arches), small jamb vaults lead to each of the round-arched openings in the inner enclosing walls. In addition, the extremely deep window walls are often very steeply slanted in order to bring the even row of windows on the outer front into alignment with the arch openings of the three oval rotundas. This, together with the skilful lighting concept, surprisingly makes it barely noticeable that the room only receives direct light from the entrance side in the west, and from the south side on the right. Because the room is in the middle of the Residence building, the windows, door windows and mezzanine windows of the left-hand long wall and the choir wall either open onto corridors or were closed immediately with mirror glass (some of them altered later).

Function

The clear emphasis on the two-storey structure in the architecture of the chapel originates in its function as a court chapel. Separated from the court, the prince-bishops could follow the Mass from the west gallery that is decorated with the large coat of arms of Prince-Bishop Friedrich

Carl von Schönborn, or from the glassed-in north oratium that could if necessary be heated – both were easily accessible, also without using the stairs, from the adjacent Episcopal Apartment on the main floor of the Residence. Since the Court Chapel was not a parish church, it initially also had no pulpit, and there are still no confessionals. If the bishop celebrated Mass himself, he could do so at the gallery altar or at the main altar on the ground floor, where there was a single-step podium with a raised seat on it beneath the north oratory.

Altars

Most of the chapel's furnishings, which are closely integrated with the architecture, was the joint accomplishment of the Würzburg court artists. The altar table in front of the colonnade of choir columns is flanked by marble sculptures of the Franconian apostle Kilian and the first Würzburg Bishop Burkhard. Like the four auxiliary figures of the side altars, these sculptures were made from designs by Johann Wolfgang van der Auwera by Italian sculptors in Carrara and delivered in 1743. The stucco-worker Antonio Bossi created the three-dimensional figures of Christ on the cross with St Mary Magdalene and putti at his feet, which are set against a blue background between the central columns on the end wall of the choir. Above the gallery a further altar continues this theme. The stucco sculpture of Mary Immaculate, also in a blue niche, and the gilded baldachin gloriole above with the Holy Trinity, accompanied by angels and putti, are also by Antonio Bossi. In addition, he and his atelier created the stucco-work allegories of the virtues over the side altars, as well as the incredibly rich stucco ornamentation of the entire chapel.

The original paintings of the side altars were produced in 1736 by Federico Bencovich but are no longer in existence. They were in fact already replaced in 1752 by altarpieces

painted by Giovanni Battista Tiepolo during the winter break in January and February, when it was too cold to paint the fresco in the Imperial Hall, or rather, too cold for the application of the plaster ground. 'The Fall of the Angels' and the 'Assumption of Mary', each 5.70 m high and 2.50 m wide, are extremely powerful scenes, magnificent examples of the Venetian's brilliant use of colour and dramatic skill. The two side altars are framed by marble sculptures from Carrara which were designed by Auwera, the left-hand altar featuring the Archangel Gabriel with a lily and Raphael with the boy Toby and the right-hand one the canonized Emperor Henry II, the founder of the bishopric of Bamberg, and his wife St Kunigunde.

Mary Magdalene and two putti at the foot of the cross behind the main altar, stucco sculptures by A. Bossi, 1740–1741

Ceiling painting

The ceiling paintings, which are not real frescoes but secco paintings, were created by the then 75-year-old court painter Rudolf Byss in 1735–1736, together with his pupils Anton Joseph Högler and Johann Thalhofer. Above the main altar is the 'Martyrdom of the Franconian apostles Kilian, Kolonat and Totnan', in the middle dome the 'Coronation of Mary', in the adjacent spandrel vaults the four Evangelists and above the music gallery the 'Triumph of Archangel Michael at the Fall of the Angels'. Although the chapel's vaulting survived the bombing of Würzburg in 1945, during the Second World War, the roof above it was destroyed by fire and the damp that penetrated as a result badly damaged both the already blackened ceiling paintings and the stucco-work. By 1963 the ceiling paintings had been restored by the artist Karl Körner, who reconstructed most of the pictures, also by overpainting them. The most recent restoration of the ceiling paintings and the stucco-work was carried out in 2009–2012.

Other furnishing

The pews were made between 1744 and 1751 by Ferdinand Hund. The carved decoration of the oak portal wings is by Paul Egell, the artistic fittings and locks by the court locksmith Georg Oegg. As mentioned above, the pulpit was only installed later on, in 1774–1775 under Prince-Bishop Adam Friedrich von Seinsheim. However, this work with reliefs and putti by Antonio's nephew Materno Bossi, who departed here from his usual Early Neoclassical style, blends in perfectly with the chapel interior, even though this is over 30 years older.

Appraisal

With the high artistic quality of its interior and decoration, the Court Chapel of the Würzburg Residence is one of the most perfect 18th-century religious buildings in Germany.

With the curved ground plan consisting of three oval rotundas and the unusual vault forms, Balthasar Neumann succeeded in welding the adjacent and intersecting sections of the room into a harmonious, highly diverse whole. In this way he contributed to the development of fluid architectural spaces that had begun in the Italian High Baroque era with the architects Guarino Guarini and Francesco Borromini and spread to Franconia and Bohemia via the Dientzenhofer architect family. With the Würzburg Court Chapel and his famous late works in Vierzehnheiligen and Neresheim, Neumann was one of the great church architects of the Baroque age.

Apart from Lucas von Hildebrandt, who was responsible for the side altars, and Tiepolo who painted the outstanding altarpieces, it was primarily Würzburg court artists, namely the sculptor Johann Wolfgang van der Auwera, the painter Rudolf Byss and the stucco-worker Antonio Bossi, who created the high-quality interior, coordinated and directed by Neumann. Bossi's contribution to the overwhelming effect of the chapel cannot be overestimated. With his atelier he completed not only the numerous gilded stucco ornaments and reliefs that decorate all the white areas, but also all the three-dimensional figures and busts of white stucco lustro and the gilded stucco capitals and the colourful stucco marble of the columns, entablature and structural elements.

Martin von Wagner Museum of the University of Würzburg

(Access from inner courtyard)

The south wing of the Residence is the location of one of the most important university museums in Europe. Its outstanding collections of ancient and post-ancient art document six millennia of art and art history.

Franz Joseph Fröhlich, Professor of Rhetoric, put together a collection of pictures for the university that in 1832 acquired the name 'Ästhetisches Attribut' ('Aesthetic Attribute'). In 1834 he received various works from the former 'Natural History and Art Cabinet' of the Minorite father and naturalist Bonavita Blank and a year later, sixty paintings from the collection of the Carthusian father Benedikt Weber. In 1857 Johann Martin von Wagner (1777–1858), an artist from Würzburg, donated the art collection he had assembled while working as the art agent of the Bavarian crown in Rome, which included 5,600 ancient objects, 10,000 drawings, 20,000 prints and 36 paintings. In 1862 Fröhlich also left his private art collection to the university. It included approximately 300 paintings, many works from the Golden Age of Dutch art among them. Since 1872 (acquisition of the Feoli Collection in Rome), Würzburg has had the third-largest collection of Greek vases in Germany. The museum continues to grow through private donations. The Graphics Collection on the same floor as the art gallery houses around 17,000 hand drawings and around 15,000 graphic reproductions.

Egyptian mummy mask from Hawara (Fayum)?, 1st century BC (fig. 1)

ANTIQUITIES COLLECTION

Famous amongst experts all over the world for its large quantity of Greek painted vases, the collection on the 3rd floor has exhibits from ancient Mediterranean cultures, primarily from Egypt, Greece and Italy. The wide spectrum of material from around four millennia ranges from precious cloth and coins to marble sculpture. The large numbers of artefacts, especially those relating to banquets, veneration of the gods and commemoration of the dead, frequently provide evidence of intensive contact and even an exchange of ideas between the various cultures.

Findings from Egyptian tombs

The series of colourful mummy-covers is a particularly interesting feature of this large collection of objects documenting traditional Egyptian ways of preparing the dead for their journey into the next world (fig. 1). Under the later influence of the Greeks and Romans the idealized faces on the covers gradually gave way to more realistic portraits. The mummy of a cat is evidence of the custom that in special cases even animals were prepared for eternal life.

Precious items from the Bronze and Iron Ages

This collection of valuable individual exhibits illustrates the broad spectrum of cultures that populated the Eastern Mediterranean and the Middle East. It includes Minoan ceramics and a Mycenaean boar's tusk helmet dating back to the prehistoric Aegean era to which Homer's epics constantly refer. A Cycladic marble idol of charming, almost modern elegance indicates the prosperity of the islands in the centre of the Aegean, which conducted a flourishing trade in raw materials. Fragments of bronze implements and weapons, some of them decorated with figures, also testify to the manual skills of the ancient peoples in Syria, East Anatolia and south-west Iran (Luristan).

Chalice from Chios: orientalizing animal frieze, late 7th century BC (fig. 2)

Vessels from the Geometric and Orientalizing period

Named after its original decor, which is derived from basic geometric shapes, the late phase of this period (c. 760–700 BC) produced the first images of animals and people after the so-called Dark Ages. These images point to gender roles within the aristocratic elites, showing men fighting and hunting and women performing charming round dances. Horses were an important status symbol. In the 7th century BC, the Greek polis flourished as a result of intensive trade relations with other nations bordering the Mediterranean. The typical oriental frieze of animals identifies the origin of the chalice with wafer-thin walls (fig. 2) as the rich island of Chios, although it was actually found in a tomb in central Italy.

Black-figure pots from the Archaic period

In the 6th and 5th centuries, Athens dominated the pottery trade in the Mediterranean with tableware painted with large-scale depictions of myths and everyday life. Initially the figures were black on a light ground and the details of the bodies and attributes were incised into the clay. This technique is represented for example by an amphora showing the hero Aeneas with his small son Ascanios and old father Anchises fleeing from burning Troy. This motif was later to become very important to the Romans, since they attributed the founding of their capital to Aeneas's descendants, as described in Virgil's great epic the *Aeneid*. This vessel was also found in Tuscany, so could have been specifically commissioned by an Etruscan from the Attic suppliers. Further exhibits show that such imports did not meet the needs of the Etruscans, who began to make vessels themselves in imitation of Greek pottery. Thus, although they took over the stories as well, their own gods and heroes also appear with increasing frequency.

Red-figure vases from the Classical period

The tableware of the Classical period now had red figures on a black ground, which was due to a change in painting techniques that had already taken place in the late 6th century. Since drawings were now made positively, details such as folds in clothes became much finer and more precise. This is demonstrated, for example by a pelike from around 460 BC, with the personified north wind (Boreas) pursuing the Attic princess Oreithyia. The man from the frosty north is normally portrayed as a barbarian. Here, however, his appearance is civilized, and the city goddess Athena is making no attempt to save the young woman she is supposed to be protecting. The reason for this is probably the support the Athenians received in the form

of a storm from the north which sank the Persian fleet close to Cape Artemision. Another scene on a stamnos from the same period (fig. 3) showing the killing of the brother of the last tyrant of Athens, Hipparchos, has more explicit historical origins. This murder for personal motives during the Panathenaic festival of 514 BC was subsequently equated by the Athenians with the birth of democracy, which is why statues were erected in honour of the two perpetrators, Harmodios and Aristogeiton, in the middle of the agora. The vase painting shows the assailants in the same pose as their statues. Such clear references to contemporary history are very rare on Greek tableware. The Antiquities Collection also includes a number of unique exhibits with rare illustrations from the world of Greek theatre, which was particularly popular in the Late Classical period (4th century BC) in the area of Magna Graecia (Sicily and Lower Italy). The image on the shoulder of an Attic hydria is a persiflage of the mythical en-

Attic red figure stamnos: The tyrant slayers, formerly in the Feoli Collection, c. 470 BC (fig. 3)

counter between Oedipus and the (Egyptian) sphinx that laid siege to his home town of Thebes and killed everyone who could not solve her riddle. Instead of the tragic hero it shows the Theban council of elders in the form of clueless Silens who are evidently not equipped for the task. This vase painting is probably a reference to a lost satyr play by the great tragedian Aeschylus, which was premiered in Athens in 467 BC.

Circular altar from the villa of Sallust: allegories of the four seasons, Rome, c. 40 AD (fig. 4)

Reliefs and three-dimensional sculptures from the Greek and Roman world

The so-called Marble Hall of the Antiquities Collection contains a combination of Greek and Roman sculptures as well as Roman copies of Greek originals. The inconspicuous head of a bearded man in relief turns out on closer inspection to be a fragment of architectural decoration from the most famous temple of the ancient world, the Parthenon on the Acropolis of Athens. It is actually one of the centaurs depicted in a battle with the Lapiths (animal-like monsters fighting civilized wedding guests) on the South Metopes of the temple. It was only in 1897 that the Dresden archaeologist Georg Treu discovered the origins of this fragment in Martin von Wagner's possession when he compared it with a plaster cast of the slab in the British Museum in London. The altar with depictions of the four seasons in the form of small putti (fig. 4) also has famous origins. It once stood in the gardens of the historian Sallust in north-east Rome, which at the time in question had just been acquired by the Roman emperor. Inspired by Greek altars in circular form with relief ornamentation, it sets the winged boys with the fruits and products of each season against a grand backdrop of candelabras with drapery hung between them. At the time, the altar was the showpiece of Roman garden furniture, which was frequently intended to evoke the idyll of sacred groves.

Central panel of the Triptych by Gherardo Starnina, Florence, c. 1400 (fig. 5)

PICTURE GALLERY

The gallery on the 2nd floor possesses around 900 paintings, about half of which are on display, together with sculptures ranging from carved Romanesque to Expressionist works. The following is a description of the most important groups of works and the highlights of the collection.

Early Italian painting

The small, three-winged portable altar with scenes from the life of Mary, possibly a work by Bernardo Daddi, and John the Baptist by Maso di Banco are examples of Florentine art from the first half of the 14th century. – The Triptych by Gherardo Starnina (c. 1400) is a particularly attractive work with its skilful composition and pure, luminous colours (fig. 5).

Medieval painting and sculpture

The Romanesque wooden figure of a saint or a prophet was probably created in the late 12th century in North Italy, possibly by a sculptor from the circle of Benedetto Antelami. – The Madonna of the Crescent Moon (fig. 6) and the Lamentation of Christ by Tilman Riemenschneider (c. 1460–1531), whose sensitive figures have a typically melancholy, longing expression, are highlights of the collection of Late Gothic carvings. – On the central panel of the three-winged altar (c. 1490) is the martyrdom of the Franconian apostles Kilian, Kolonat and Totnan; in the background Marienberg Fortress before it was substantially rebuilt in the 16th century.

Tilman Riemenschneider, Madonna (detail), after 1503 (fig. 6)

Dutch and German painting 1500–1600

The Portrait of Christ with the crown of thorns by Aelbrecht Bouts (c. 1500) arouses the observer's compassion ('compassio') with its narrow focus. – Hans Schäufelein, who worked between 1503 and 1507 in Albrecht Dürer's atelier, created the portrait of the imperial official Sixtus Oelhafen in around 1503. – The Battle Scene dated 1514 is an outstanding example of German Renaissance depiction. – Lukas Cranach the Elder's Man of Sorrows was painted in the Reformation era (after 1537). – The style of the Italian High Renaissance is reflected by the depiction of Eve by Frans Floris I from around 1550 and the somewhat later Susanna at Her Bath by Willem Key. – The International Mannerism style cultivated from around 1600 at the court of Emperor Rudolf II in Prague is represented by Hans von Aachen (St Sebastian) and Bartholomäus Spranger (Presentation at the Temple).

Bernardino Licinio, Artist Friends in a Mirror, c. 1530 (fig. 7)

Painting from the Italian Renaissance and Early Baroque period

The Madonna by Bernardino dei Conti was painted in around 1500 in Milan, and was influenced by Leonardo da Vinci. – The large circular picture shows the Holy Family with the Infant St John the Baptist: the type and style of the picture are characteristic of Florentine painting shortly after 1500. – The Double Portrait of Artist Friends in a Mirror is attributed to Bernardino Licinio and dated around 1530 (fig. 7). With its complicated mirror setting it is probably to be interpreted as a call to self-knowledge. – Luca Cambiaso from Genoa painted the cabinet picture of Venus Disarming Cupid in around the mid-16th century. – The Madonna by Giulio Cesare Proccacini (early 17th century) combines Mannerist and Early Baroque elements. – Orazio Borgianni's St Christopher (c. 1605) is based on the style of Caravaggio.

The relief by Hans van der Mulen shows an early portrait of Julius Echter in an architectural setting (1576). The Würzburg prince-bishop appears in secular clothing. – Zacharias Juncker the Elder's alabaster statues, made in around 1610 for the Würzburg Cartreuse Engelgarten (Angel Garden) have the typical characteristics of German Renaissance sculpture. The Ecstasy of St Francis by the same sculptor from around 1620–1630 has a more 'Baroque' character. – Hans Ulrich Bühler's interior of Würzburg Cathedral (1627) shows the church as it looked after it had been refurbished under Echter.

Italian and French painting from the High and Late Baroque epochs

François de Nomé, who came from Metz but worked in Naples, specialized in imaginary architecture (Christ and the Woman Taken in Adultery, 1610–1620). – The Penitent Mary Magdalene was painted by Nicolas Régnier in around 1620 in Rome and influenced by the Italian Early Baroque style. – The Bacchanal by Giovanni Battista Gaulli called Baciccio (c. 1675) is typical of figure painting in the Roman High Baroque style. – The monumental Abduction of Europe is an early work by Luca Giordano (c. 1660). In his later years the Neapolitan created the emotional Raising of the Cross (c. 1690). – In St Veronica by Giuseppe Chiari (2nd half of the 17th century), the Baroque formal language is noticeably less evident, and the emotion internalized. – The Quirinal Palace with the departure of Pope Innocent XII by Gaspar van Wittel called Vanvitelli (1693) is a magnificent architecture veduta. – The painting of Susanna and the Elders by the Venetian Giovanni Antonio Pellegrini, possibly painted when he was staying in Würzburg in 1724, marks the transition to the Rococo period. – This contrasts with the Late

Baroque, visionary portrayal of St Anthony Preaching to the Fish by Alessandro Magnasco from Genoa (†1749). – The history paintings of Mucius Scaevola Before Porsenna and Coriolanus and the Roman Women were created by Giovanni Battista Tiepolo during his Würzburg years (1750–1753), probably for Balthasar Neumann. They present the Roman virtues of fortitude and magnanimity with magnificent use of colour. – The ruin landscapes by Francesco Guardi (c. 1760) are 'capriccios', compositions with imaginary architecture and 'meaningless' figure staffages.

17th-century Dutch painting

The Flower Still Life by Andries Daniels (c. 1600) portrays flowers from different seasons as a symbol of time and transience. – Genre and still life elements are combined in the Vegetable Seller by Adriaen van Utrecht (c. 1620–1630). – The small-format Seascape with Fishermen by Willem van Diest (1643) is typical of the 'tonal phase' of Dutch painting. – With its bright 'southern' light, the picture of St Jerome in the Forest (1646) by Nicolaes Berchem shows Italian influence. – The Still Life with Wine Glasses, Lemon, Bread Roll and Caviar by Pieter Claesz (1640) makes stunning use of refractions and reflections. – In Jupiter and Callisto, Frans Wouters (c. 1642– 1645) depicts the abduction of the nymph by the father of the gods, who has temporarily disguised himself as her mistress Diana.

German art of the Baroque and Neoclassical period

Anton Faistenberger's penchant for the heroic landscape is illustrated by his Coastal and Mountain Landscapes (late 17th century). – The portrait of a young woman (mid-18th century) recently attributed to Christian Seybold displays a frivolity typical of the Rococo age. – In 1765 Franz Anton Ermeltraut painted the lively portrait of

Max Liebermann,
Girl Sewing
(Study for Free
Period in the
Amsterdam
Orphanage),
1881
(fig. 8)

an artist, possibly the Würzburg court stucco-worker Materno Bossi. – The Rape of the Sabine Women by Christoph Fesel (1801) combines characteristics of the Late Baroque period and French Neoclassicism. – The early work of Martin von Wagner shows that he was very receptive to the tendencies of European art in around 1800. His monumental Council of the Greeks outside Troy (1807) reflects the international style of Neoclassicism. The bust of Wagner is the work of an unknown German-Roman sculptor from around 1820.

19th-century painting

The Portrait of Max I Joseph, King of Bavaria, by Bonavita Blank and Barbara Thein (c. 1820) is made entirely of feathers. It is the only surviving example of Blank's 'mosaic paintings', for which only natural materials were used. – Johann Friedrich Kreul painted the authentic portrait of Kaspar Hauser (1830) in the Biedermeier style. – Joseph Being Sold by His Brothers by Carl Gottlieb Peschel (1831) is a typical example of Nazarene art. – The landscape around Rome is portrayed by Carl Rottmann as an elegiac history landscape (Campagna near Ponte Nomentano, c. 1830), by Johann Wilhelm Schirmer as an Arcadian place of yearning (Roman Campagna with Ruins of an Aqueduct, c. 1847) and by Karl Lindemann-Frommel as an atmospheric play (Roman Campagna from the Via Appia, 1866). – The Girl Sewing by Max Liebermann (1881) is an Impressionistic study of fleeting light effects (fig. 8). – In the Portrait of Ignaz Döllinger, Franz von Lenbach shows the intellectual striving of the famous theologian (1880s).

Classical Modernism

With his Blind Beggar (model 1906, porcelain cast 1912), Ernst Barlach portrayed neediness and poverty in an existential way. – Expressionism and New Objectivity meet in

the Forest Landscape by Willy Jaeckel (1923) and the
View of the Staffelsee by Hans Otto Baumann (1932). –
The Young Woman With a Basket by Emy Roeder was
created in 1940 in Florence, where the sculptress whose
work was labeled 'degenerate' had found refuge. Here she
also met the Matisse pupil Hans Purrmann (View of St
Ilario and Monte Morcello, 1938–1940).

Veitshöchheim Palace and Court Garden

Veitshöchheim Palace and Court Garden

Veitshöchheim Palace, only eight kilometres down the River Main from Würzburg, is surrounded by one of the most important Rococo gardens in Germany. Until 1802 it was the summer seat of the Würzburg prince-bishops. The summer palace was created from 1680 to 1682 under Prince-Bishop Peter Philipp von Dernbach from a hunting lodge and was extended from 1749 to 1753 by Balthasar Neumann. The ceiling stucco-work by Antonio Bossi also dates from this period. The highlights of the interior are the prince-bishop's apartment and the rooms furnished in around 1810 for Grand Duke Ferdinand

Nobleman as a putto playing the flute (below)

of Tuscany. On the ground floor is a permanent exhibition documenting the history of the Court Garden. The transformation of the palace grounds into an ornamental pleasure garden was begun in 1702 by Prince-Bishop Johann Philipp von Greiffenclau with the creation of terraces and lakes. The garden was redesigned in its present Rococo form under Adam Friedrich von Seinsheim, who reigned from 1755 to 1779. It is populated by over 200 sculptures by the Würzburg court sculptors Johann Wolfgang van der Auwera, Ferdinand Tietz and Johann Peter Wagner.

Selected bibliography

OFFICIAL GUIDES

BESCHREIBUNG UND GESCHICHTE DER KÖNIGLICHEN SCHLÖSSER UND LUSTGÄRTEN von Würzburg, Aschaffenburg, Veitshöchheim, Werneck und Bad Brückenau im Unter-Main-Kreise des Königreich's Bayern, von JAKOB MAY, Königl. Bayr. Obersthofmarschall-Stabs-Assessor vorbenannter kgl. Residenzen, Würzburg 1830, pp. 1–49

OFFIZIELLER FÜHRER durch das Kgl. Schloß Würzburg. Herausgegeben und verlegt vom Kgl. Oberstabssekretär G. FRIEDRICH LECHLER, Schloßverwalter in Würzburg, Würzburg 1914 (auch auf Französisch und Englisch; 12. deutsche Auflage 1928)

RESIDENZMUSEUM IN WÜRZBURG. Kleiner Führer, herausgegeben von der Direktion der Museen und Kunstsammlungen des ehemaligen Kronguts. Bearbeitet von HEINRICH KREISEL, München 1924

RESIDENZ WÜRZBURG. Amtlicher Führer. Bearbeitet von HEINRICH KREISEL. Bayerische Verwaltung der staatlichen Schlösser, Gärten und Seen, München 1933 (dritte und letzte Auflage 1939)

RESIDENZ WÜRZBURG UND HOFGARTEN. (Amtlicher Führer). Bearbeitet von ERICH BACHMANN. Erste Nachkriegsauflage, München 1970; zweite Nachkriegsauflage 1971; zweite (3.) erweiterte Nachkriegsauflage 1973; zweite (4.) nochmals erweiterte Nachkriegsauflage mit Verzeichnis der Staatsgalerie von ROLF KULTZEN 1975; dritte (5.) Nachkriegsauflage 1976; vierte (6.) Nachkriegsauflage 1978; fünfte (7.) Nachkriegsauflage 1980; sechste (8.) Nachkriegsauflage 1981

RESIDENZ WÜRZBURG UND HOFGARTEN. Amtlicher Führer. Bearbeitet von ERICH BACHMANN und BURKARD VON RODA, Verzeichnis der Staatsgalerie von ROLF KULTZEN. Neunte, erweiterte Nachkriegsauflage (revidierte Zählung), München 1982; zehnte, ergänzte Auflage 1988; zwölfte, um das Martin von Wagner Museum erweiterte Auflage 1994; dreizehnte, neu gestaltete Auflage 2001; vierzehnte Auflage 2015

THE WÜRZBURG RESIDENCE AND COURT GARDENS, 13th english edition, München 2015 (corresponds to the fourteenth postwar German edition 2015)

LA RÉSIDENCE ET LES JARDINS DE WURTZBOURG, 7ème édition française, München 2007 (entspricht der dreizehnten deutschen Nachkriegsauflage 2001)

LA RESIDENZA E IL GIARDINO DI CORTE DI WÜRZBURG, terza edizione italiana, München 2015 (entspricht der vierzehnten deutschen Nachkriegsauflage 2015)

LA RESIDENCIA Y SUS JARDINES WÜRZBURG, primera edición español, München 2005 (entspricht der dreizehnten deutschen Nachkriegsauflage 2001)

LITERATURE ON THE BUILDING AND ITS FURNISHINGS (CHRONOLOGICAL)

FELIX MADER: Die Kunstdenkmäler des Königreichs Bayern, 3. Bd., Unterfranken und Aschaffenburg, XII Stadt Würzburg, München 1915, pp. 413–498

GEORG ECKERT: Balthasar Neumann und die Würzburger Residenzpläne. Ein Beitrag zur Entwicklungsgeschichte des Würzburger Residenzbaues, Straßburg 1917

HEINRICH GÖBEL: Würzburg und Fulda. Ein Beitrag zur Geschichte der deutschen Wirkteppichmanufakturen im 18. Jahrhundert. In: Der Cicerone 12, 1920, pp. 818–823 and pp. 848–856

KARL LOHMEYER: Die Briefe Balthasar Neumanns an Friedrich Karl von Schönborn, Saarbrücken 1921

HEINRICH GÖBEL: Das Brüsseler Wirkergeschlecht der van der Hecke. In: Der Cicerone 14, 1922, pp. 16–31

HEINRICH KREISEL: Die künstlerischen Ausstattungen des Hauptstockes der fürstbischöflichen Residenz zu Würzburg, Diss. phil. ungedr., Würzburg 1922

RICHARD SEDLMAIER und RUDOLF PFISTER: Die fürstbischöfliche Residenz zu Würzburg, München 1923

HEINRICH KREISEL: Carl Maximilian Mattern, ein Würzburger Kunstschreiner des 18. Jahrhunderts. In: Der Cicerone 15, 1923, pp. 413–419

HEINRICH KREISEL: Die Alexanderwirkteppiche in der Würzburger Residenz. In: Münchner Jahrbuch der bildenden Kunst, N.F. Bd. II, 1925, pp. 227–249

FRIEDRICH H. HOFMANN: Das Ehrenhofgitter der Residenz in Würzburg. In: Zeitschrift für Denkmalpflege 2, 1927/28, pp. 171–187

HEINRICH KREISEL: Ein verschollener Hausaltar der Würzburger Residenz. In: Archiv des Historischen Vereins von Unterfranken und Aschaffenburg 68, 1929, pp. 520–523

HEINRICH KREISEL: Die Kunstschätze der Würzburger Residenz, Würzburg 1930

ADOLF FEULNER: Die Toskanazimmer der Würzburger Residenz. In: Zeitschrift für Kunstgeschichte 3, 1934, pp. 104–108

CATHARINA BOELCKE-ASTOR: Der Frühklassizismus, seine Ursachen und seine Entwicklung bei J. P. Wagner (1730–1809), Diss. masch., Frankfurt 1941

THEODOR HETZER: Die Fresken Tiepolos in der Würzburger Residenz, Frankfurt 1943

HEINRICH KREISEL: Die Würzburger Gobelinmanufaktur und ihre Erzeugnisse. In: Mainfränkisches Jahrbuch für Geschichte und Kunst 4, 1952, pp. 151–175

MAX H. VON FREEDEN: Balthasar Neumann, Gedächtnisschau zum 200. Todestage, Ausstellungskatalog, Würzburg 1953, Residenz Würzburg

ERICH BACHMANN: Balthasar Neumann und das Mittelalter, Stifterjahrbuch III, 1953, p. 134

MAX H. VON FREEDEN: Quellen zur Geschichte des Barocks in Franken unter dem Einfluß des Hauses Schönborn, I. Teil: Die Zeit des Erzbischofs Lothar Franz und des Bischofs Johann Philipp Franz von Schönborn 1693–1729, 2. Halbband, Würzburg 1955

MAX H. VON FREEDEN und CARL LAMB: Das Meisterwerk des Giovanni Battista Tiepolo (Die Fresken der Würzburger Residenz), München 1956

LUDWIG DÖRY: Würzburger Wirkereien und ihre Vorbilder, In: Mainfränkisches Jahrbuch für Geschichte und Kunst 12, 1960, pp. 189–216

FRITZ ZINCK: Kulturdokumente Frankens aus dem Germanischen Nationalmuseum, Bamberg 1961

CHRISTIAN BAUER: Der Würzburger Hofgarten, In: Mainfränkisches Jahrbuch für Geschichte und Kunst 13, 1961, pp. 1–31

WALTER SCHERZER: Das Staatsarchiv 200 Jahre in der Residenz. In: Mainfränkisches Jahrbuch für Geschichte und Kunst 18, 1966, pp. 189–198

CHARLES EDWARD MAYER: The Staircase of the Episcopal Palace at Würzburg, Diss. University of Michigan 1967

ERICH BACHMANN: Die Würzburger Residenz. In: Weltkunst 40, 1970, pp. 375

HEINRICH KREISEL: Die Kunst des deutschen Möbel, Bd. II, München 1970

PETER KOLB: Die Wappen der Würzburger Fürstbischöfe, Würzburg 1974

GERDA ZIMMERMANN: Der Hofstaat der Fürstbischöfe von Würzburg von 1648 bis 1803, Dissertation Würzburg 1976

MARK ASHTON: Allegory, Fact and Meaning in Giambattista Tiepolo's, Four Continents in Würzburg. In: Art Bulletin 60, 1978, pp. 109–125

GABRIELE DISCHINGER: Die Würzburger Residenz im ausgehenden 18. Jahrhundert, Wiesbaden 1978
–: Der Residenzplatz zu Würzburg – Entwürfe für die Kolonnaden. In: Mainfränkisches Jahrbuch für Geschichte und Kunst 30, 1978, pp. 93–97

ALBRECHT MILLER: Die Residenz in Würzburg, Königstein im Taunus 1978 (4. Auflage 2008)

BURKARD VON RODA: »Laque Martin« in Franken. In: Jahrbuch der bayerischen Denkmalpflege 32, 1978, pp. 185–188

HANS REUTHER: Die Zeichnungen aus dem Nachlaß Balthasar Neumanns. Der Bestand in der Kunstbibliothek Berlin. Veröffentlichung der Kunstbibliothek Berlin, Bd. 82, Berlin 1979

FRANK BÜTTNER: Die Sonne Frankens. Ikonographie des Freskos der Würzburger Residenz. In: Münchner Jahrbuch der bildenden Kunst, 3. Folge, Bd. 30, 1979, pp. 159–186
–: Giovanni Battista Tiepolo. Die Fresken in der Residenz zu Würzburg, Würzburg 1980

KARL SCHÄFER: Johann Prokop Mayer 1735–1804. Ein Würzburger Hofgärtner. In: Mainfränkisches Jahrbuch für Geschichte und Kunst 32, 1980, pp. 165–176

BURKARD VON RODA: Adam Friedrich von Seinsheim, Auftraggeber zwischen Rokoko und Klassizismus. Zur Würzburger und Bamberger Hofkunst anhand der Privatkorrespondenz des Fürstbischofs (1755–1779). Quellen und Darstellungen zur fränkischen Kunstgeschichte, Bd. 6, Neustadt/Aisch 1980

MAX H. VON FREEDEN: Balthasar Neumann, Leben und Werk, 3. Auflage, München 1981

JOACHIM HOTZ: Das »Skizzenbuch Balthasar Neumann«. Studien zur Arbeitsweise des Würzburger Meisters und zur Dekorationskunst im 18. Jahrhundert, 2 Bde., Wiesbaden 1981

HANS-PETER TRENSCHEL: Meisterwerke fränkischer Möbelkunst. Carl Maximilian Mattern, Würzburg 1982

HANS REUTHER: Balthasar Neumann. Der mainfränkische Barockbaumeister, München 1983

ROBERT MÜNSTER: Die Melodien einer Bamberger Pendule aus dem Jahre 1750. In: Musik in Bayern, Heft 26, 1983, pp. 29–34

BURKARD VON RODA: Der Frankoniabrunnen auf dem Würzburger Residenzplatz. In: Jahrbuch für fränkische Landesforschung 43, 1983, pp. 195–214

–: Höfische Interieurs. Innenräume des Rokoko und Empire aus der Residenz Würzburg. In: Kunst und Antiquitäten, 1984, Heft 6, pp. 44–51

ERICH HUBALA und OTTO MAYER: Die Residenz zu Würzburg, Würzburg 1984

ERICH HUBALA: Genie, Kollektiv und Meisterschaft – zur Autorenfrage der Würzburger Residenzarchitektur. In: Martin Gosebruch zu Ehren. Hrsg. von Frank Neidhart Steigerwald, München 1984, pp. 157–170

IRENE HELMREICH-SCHOELLER: Empiremöbel in Würzburg. Sitzgarnituren aus den ehemaligen Toskanazimmern der Residenz. In: Kunst und Antiquitäten, 1985, Heft 3, pp. 60–66

HANS REUTHER: Die Konstruktion der Treppenarme im Stiegenhaus der Würzburger Residenz. In: Intuition und Darstellung. Erich Hubala zum 24. März 1985. Hrsg. von Frank Büttner und Christian Lenz, München 1985, pp. 241–250

BURKARD VON RODA: Aus Würzburger Hofbesitz, Säkularisationsgut in Münchner Sammlungen. In: Kunst und Antiquitäten, 1985, Heft 3, pp. 52–59

–: »Das Spiegelzimmer im königlichen Schloß zu Würzburg.« An interior painted by Georg Dehn and a report by Georg Dollmann commissioned by Ludwig II of Bavaria. In: Furniture History 21, 1985, pp. 107–120

WILFRIED HANSMANN: Balthasar Neumann – Leben und Werk, Köln 1986

BERNHARD SCHÜTZ: Balthasar Neumann, Freiburg 1986

IRENE HELMREICH–SCHOELLER: Die Toskanazimmer der Würzburger Residenz, München 1987

HANS-PETER TRENSCHEL: Das Spiegelkabinett der Würzburger Residenz. In: Altfränkische Bilder und Wappenkalender 86, Würzburg 1987, pp. 15–19

AUS BALTHASAR NEUMANNS BAUBÜRO: Pläne der Sammlung Eckert zu Bauten des großen Barockarchitekten. Sonderausstellung aus Anlaß der 300. Wiederkehr des Geburtstages Balthasar Neumanns. Mainfränkisches Museum Würzburg. Ausstellungskatalog, Würzburg 1987

SAMMLUNG ECKERT. Plansammlung aus dem Nachlaß Balthasar Neumanns im Mainfränkischen Museum Würzburg. Unter Mitverwendung der Vorarbeiten von Joachim Hotz bearbeitet von Hanswernfried Muth, Elisabeth Sperzel und Hans-Peter Trenschel. Mainfränkisches Museum Würzburg (Hrsg.), Würzburg 1987

STEFAN KUMMER: Balthasar Neumann und die frühe Planungsphase der Würzburger Residenz. In: Balthasar Neumann, Beiträge zum Jubiläumsjahr 1987. Hrsg. von Thomas Korth und Joachim Poeschke, München 1987, pp. 79–91

BERNHARD SCHÜTZ: Fassaden als Weltarchitektur. Die Würzburger Residenz. In: Balthasar Neumann, Beiträge zum Jubiläumsjahr 1987. Hrsg. von Thomas Korth und Joachim Poeschke, München 1987, pp. 92–112

ANNEGRET VON LÜDE: Studien zum Bauwesen in Würzburg 1720 bis 1750, Würzburg 1987

STEFAN KUMMER: Das Spiegelkabinett der Würzburger Residenz. In: Würzburg-heute 45, 1988, pp. 53–57

BARBARA STRIEDER: Johann Zick (1702–1762) – Die Fresken und Deckengemälde, Worms 1990

KATHARINA FEGG: Die fürstbischöfliche Wandteppichmanufaktur zu Würzburg 1721–1779. In: Mainfränkisches Jahrbuch für Geschichte und Kunst 43, 1991, pp. 8–79

VERENA FRIEDRICH: Johann Georg Oegg: Die schmiedeeisernen Gitter der Fürstbischöflichen Residenz zu Würzburg, Würzburg 1993

BERND M. MAYER: Johann Rudolf Bys (1662–1738) – Studien zu Leben und Werk, München 1994

SVETLANA ALPERS und MICHAEL BAXANDALL: Tiepolo and the Pictorial Intelligence, New Haven/London 1994 (deutsch: Tiepolo oder die Intelligenz der Malerei, Berlin 1996)

KATALOG DER AUSSTELLUNG: Der Himmel auf Erden – Tiepolo in Würzburg, 2 Bde. Hrsg. von PETER O. KRÜCKMANN, München/New York 1996

PETER O. KRÜCKMANN: Heaven on Earth: Tiepolo, Masterpieces of the Würzburg Years, Munich/New York 1996 (deutsch: Tiepolo: Der Triumph der Malerei im 18. Jahrhundert, München 2004)

BETTINA SCHWABE und SONJA SEIDEL: Drei Supraporten von Domenico Tiepolo. In: Restauro 102, 1996, pp. 320–327

THORSTEN MARR: Restaurierung und Wertschätzung – Giovanni Battista Tiepolo und die Fresken der Würzburger Residenz. In: Mainfränkisches Jahrbuch für Geschichte und Kunst 49, 1997, pp. 157–166

ARNO STÖRKEL: Der Mann mit dem Pferd und Neumann auf dem Kanonenrohr. Eine Studie zur Identifikation zweier Personen in Tiepolos WÜRZBURGER TREPPENHAUS. In: Mainfränkisches Jahrbuch für Geschichte und Kunst 49, 1997, pp. 141–156

JARL KREMEIER: Die Hofkirche der Würzburger Residenz, Worms 1999

IRIS VISOSKY-ANTRACK: Materno und Augustin Bossi, München/Berlin 2000

PETER STEPHAN: Im Glanz der Majestät des Reiches, Tiepolo und die Würzburger Residenz. Die Reichsidee der Schönborn und die politische Ikonologie des Barock, 2 Bde., Weißenhorn 2002

VERENA FRIEDRICH: Rokoko in der Residenz Würzburg. Studien zu Ornament und Dekoration des Rokoko in der ehemaligen fürstbischöflichen Residenz zu Würzburg, München 2004

MANFRED SCHULLER: Ein Dach am Rande des Machbaren, Balthasar Neumanns verlorenes Dachwerk über dem Treppenhaus der Würzburger Residenz. In: Alles unter einem Dach, Festschrift für Konrad Bedal. Hrsg. von Herbert May und Kilian Kreilinger, Fulda 2004, pp. 293–303

MARTIN SCHAWE: Zentral – dezentral. Die Bayerischen Staatsgemäldesammlungen in Franken. In: »200 Jahre Franken in Bayern, 1806 bis 2006«, Ausstellungskatalog, Haus der Bayerischen Geschichte, Nürnberg 2006, Aufsatzband, pp. 16–27

WERNER HELMBERGER und MATTHIAS STASCHULL: Tiepolos Welt. Das Deckenfresko im Treppenhaus der Residenz Würzburg, München 2006, 2. Aufl. 2010 (english: Tiepolo's world, Munich 2008)

JARL KREMEIER: Der königlich Vorplatz, so in 4eck zu bringen. Bemerkungen zu Lage und Gestaltung des Vorplatzes der Würzburger Residenz. In: Wiener Jahrbuch für Kunstgeschichte, LV/LVI, 2006/2007, pp. 69–81

VERENA FRIEDRICH: Der große Kronleuchter im Treppenhaus der Würzburger Residenz. Zur Geschichte eines verlorenen Ausstattungsstücks. In: Architektur und Figur. Das Zusammenspiel der Künste. Festschrift für Stefan Kummer zum 60. Geburtstag. Hrsg. von Nicole Riegel und Damian Dombrowski, München/Berlin 2007, pp. 425–439

VERENA FRIEDRICH: Pomona Franconica - Früchte für den Fürstbischof, Würzburg 2007

FRANK BÜTTNER u.a. (Hrsg.): Barock und Rokoko, Geschichte der bildenden Kunst in Deutschland, Bd. 5, München 2008

JOHANNES MACK: Der Baumeister und Architekt Joseph Greissing – Mainfränkischer Barock vor Balthasar Neumann, Würzburg 2008

196

HEIKO BRAUNGARDT: »... mithin höchst dieselbe als Kayserin zu achten
seye.« Der Besuch Maria Theresias in Würzburg im September 1745
anhand der Quellen. In: Frankenland 2009, pp. 160–174

WERNER HELMBERGER und MATTHIAS STASCHULL: Tiepolos Reich. Fresken und Raumschmuck im Kaisersaal der Residenz Würzburg, München
2009 (english: Tiepolo's empire, Munich 2015)

HANS-PETER TRENSCHEL: Johann alias Daniel Köhler und »die viel-
leicht schönste Rokokogarnitur Frankens« – mit einem Exkurs zum
bildhauerischen Werk Daniel Köhlers. In: Mainfränkisches Jahrbuch für
Geschichte und Kunst 62, 2010, pp. 123–150

STEFAN KUMMER: Kunstgeschichte der Stadt Würzburg 800–1945,
Regensburg 2011

ALEXANDER WIESNETH: Gewölbekonstruktionen Balthasar Neumanns,
Berlin/München 2011

HANS-PETER TRENSCHEL: Ein vergeblicher Griff nach den Sternen – der
Würzburger Stukkator Friedrich Manger. In: Mainfränkisches Jahrbuch
für Geschichte und Kunst 63, 2011, pp. 73–116

CHRISTINE CASEY: New light on the court chapel Würzburg. In: Decorative plasterwork in Ireland and Europe. Hrsg. von Christine Casey und
Conor Lucey, Dublin 2012, pp. 240–253

JÖRG LUSIN: Das Spiegelkabinett der Residenz Würzburg. Entstehung,
Zerstörung und Wiedergeburt, Würzburg 2015

HISTORICAL PRESERVATION, RECONSTRUCTION, RESTORATION

RUDOLF ESTERER und HEINRICH KREISEL: Instandsetzung und Ausge-
staltung der staatlichen bayerischen Schlösser in Franken. Deutsche
Kunst und Denkmalpflege, 1934, pp. 2–20 (pp. 2–7)

OTTO HERTWIG: Die Wiederherstellung der Tiepolo-Fresken in der Residenz Würzburg. Österreichische Zeitschrift für Kunst und Denkmalpflege 6, 1952, pp. 57–63

JOHN D. SKILTON JR.: Würzburg 1945, Erinnerungen eines amerikani-
schen Kunstschutz-Offiziers, Würzburg 1954

KARL KÖRNER: Zur Instandsetzung der Würzburger Hofkirche. Deutsche
Kunst und Denkmalpflege, 1962, pp. 47–52

LARS LANDSCHREIBER: Sicherung des Vestibüls, des Treppenhauses und
des Weißen Saales in der Residenz Würzburg. Deutsche Kunst und
Denkmalpflege, 1968, pp. 87–91
 –: Die neue Farbgebung im Treppenhaus der Würzburger Residenz.
Ebenda, pp. 92

OTTO MEYER: Kritik und Rechtfertigung nach 25 Jahren Wiederaufbau. Würzburg heute, Zeitschrift für Kultur und Wirtschaft, 1970, pp. 122–126

HEINRICH KREISEL: Die Wiederherstellung und Einrichtung der südlichen Paradezimmer in der Würzburger Residenz. Kunstchronik 23, 1970, pp. 173–176
–: Wiedereröffnung der »Weißen Zimmer« in der Würzburger Residenz. Kunstchronik 25, 1972, pp. 353–357

HEINZ LÜTZELBERGER: Der Wiederaufbau der Würzburger Residenz am Beispiel der Ingelheimer Zimmer und des Fürstensaals. Schönere Heimat 68, München 1979, Heft 1, pp. 15–21

ERICH HUBALA und OTTO MEYER: Die Residenz zu Würzburg, Würzburg 1984

MATTHIAS STASCHULL: Das Deckenfresko im Treppenhaus der Würzburger Residenz von Giambattista Tiepolo – Ein Beitrag zur Restaurierungsgeschichte. In: Bayerische Schlösser – Bewahren und Erforschen (= Bayerische Verwaltung der staatlichen Schlösser, Gärten und Seen, Forschungen zur Kunst- und Kulturgeschichte. Hrsg. von Gerhard Hojer, Bd. V), München 1996, pp. 289–298

MATTHIAS STASCHULL: Carl Lambs Farbaufnahmen des Tiepolo-Freskos im Treppenhaus der Würzburger Residenz (1944/45) und ihre Bedeutung für die Restaurierungen 1948–49 und 2003–06. In: »Führerauftrag Monumentalmalerei«: eine Fotokampagne 1943–1945, Veröffentlichungen des Zentralinstituts für Kunstgeschichte in München 18. Hrsg. von Christian Fuhrmeister, Köln 2006, pp. 211–220

PETER SEIBERT: Der Wiederaufbau der Residenz Würzburg als Raumkunstmuseum. In: Schloss Charlottenburg in Berlin, im Wandel denkmalpflegerischer Auffassungen, Jahrbuch der Stiftung Preußische Schlösser und Gärten Berlin-Brandenburg 7, 2005, Berlin 2007, pp. 111–119, fig. pp. 155
–: Managementplan und Pufferzone für die Residenz Würzburg, Ideen für die denkmalgerechte Entwicklung und nachhaltigen Schutz. In: Weltkulturerbe Deutschland, Präventive Konservierung und Erhaltungsperspektiven. Icomos Hefte des Deutschen Nationalkomitees XLV. Hrsg. von Ursula Schädler-Saub, Regensburg 2008, pp. 118–124

MATTHIAS STASCHULL und BERNHARD RÖSCH (Hrsg.): Die Restaurierung eines Meisterwerks – Das Tiepolo-Fresko im Treppenhaus der Würzburger Residenz, Berlin/München 2009

MATTHIAS STASCHULL: Die Hofkirche der Residenz Würzburg – Aspekte ihrer Restaurierung von 2009 bis 2012. In: UNESCO-Welterbe in Deutschland und Mitteleuropa, Bilanz und Perspektiven (Icomos Hefte des Deutschen Nationalkomitees LVII), Berlin 2014, pp. 161–170

Grand Duke Ferdinand III, full-figure state portrait by an unknown artist, c. 1810

Index of persons

Publications by the Bavarian Palace Administration

The Bavarian Palace Administration publishes official guides with colour photos on all the places of interest for which it is responsible; a number of these are available in several languages. It also offers plans of many of the parks accompanied by brief, illustrated descriptions. Exhibition catalogues and inventories, picture books and scientific works complete the varied spectrum of publications. In addition to the books there are also posters, CD-ROMs and videos on individual properties and special topics.

A complete list of publications can be ordered free of charge from the following address:

Bayerische Verwaltung der
staatlichen Schlösser, Gärten und Seen
Postfach 20 20 63 · 80020 München
Tel. +49 89 17908-0 · Fax +49 89 17908-190
shop@bsv.bayern.de · www.schloesser.bayern.de

Places of interest administered by the Bavarian Palace Administration

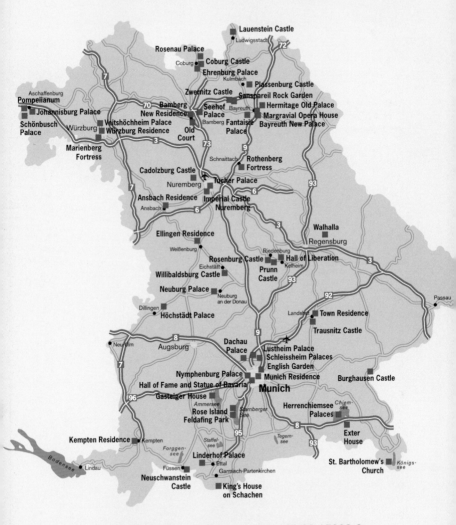

Lauenstein Castle
Ludwigstadt
72
Rosenau Palace
Coburg
Coburg Castle
Ehrenburg Palace
Kulmbach
Plassenburg Castle
Zwernitz Castle
Sanspareil Rock Garden
70
Bamberg
New Residence
Seehof
Palace
Bayreuth
Hermitage Old Palace
Margravial Opera House
Veitshöchheim Palace
Bamberg
Fantaisie
Bayreuth New Palace
Würzburg Residence
Palace
Old
Court
73
Pompeianum
Aschaffenburg
Johannisburg Palace
Schönbusch
Palace
Würzburg
Marienberg
Fortress
3
Schnaittach
Rothenberg
Fortress
9
Cadolzburg Castle
Nuremberg
Tucher Palace
93
Ansbach Residence
Imperial Castle
Nuremberg
Ansbach
6
Walhalla
Ellingen Residence
Regensburg
Weißenburg
3
Riedenburg
Rosenburg Castle
Hall of Liberation
Eichstätt
Prunn
Kelheim
Willibaldsburg Castle
Castle
93
Neuburg Palace
Neuburg
an der Donau
92
Passau
Dillingen
Landshut
Town Residence
Höchstädt Palace
Trausnitz Castle
8
9
Dachau
Palace
Augsburg
Lustheim Palace
Schleissheim Palaces
Neu-Ulm
English Garden
7
Nymphenburg Palace
Munich Residence
Burghausen Castle
Hall of Fame and Statue of Bavaria
Gasteiger House
Munich
96
Ammersee
Herrenchiemsee
Chiem-
see
Rose Island
Starnberger
Palaces
Feldafing Park
See
Kempten Residence
Kempten
Staffel-
see
Tegern-
8
see
95
Exter
House
Forggen-
see
93
Bodensee
Linderhof Palace
St. Bartholomew's
Königs-
Lindau
Füssen
Ettal
Church
see
Neuschwanstein
Garmisch-Partenkirchen
Castle
King's House
on Schachen

www.schloesser.bayern.de · Tel. +49 89 17908-0

Ansbach
- Ansbach Residence

Aschaffenburg
- Johannisburg Palace
- Pompeiianum
- Schönbusch Palace and Park

Bamberg
- New Residence in Bamberg

Bamberg/ Memmelsdorf
- Seehof Palace

Bayreuth
- New Palace
- Margravial Opera House

Bayreuth/Donndorf
- Museum of Garden Design Fantaisie Palace and Park

Bayreuth/Eremitage
- Hermitage Old Palace

Bayreuth/Wonsees-Sanspareil
- Rock Garden and Oriental Building
- Zwernitz Castle

Burghausen
- Burghausen Castle

Cadolzburg
- Castle and Castle Garden

Coburg
- Ehrenburg Palace

Coburg/Rödental
- Rosenau Palace

Dachau
- Dachau Palace

Donaustauf
- Walhalla

Eichstätt
- Willibaldsburg Castle

Ellingen
- Ellingen Residence

Feldafing/ Lake Starnberg
- Feldafing Park and Rose Island

Herrenchiemsee
- Herrenchiemsee New Palace and King Ludwig II Museum
- Museum in the Augustinian monastery Herrenchiemsee (Old Palace)

Höchstädt
- Höchstädt Palace

Holzhausen
- Gasteiger House

Kelheim
- Hall of Liberation

Kempten
- Kempten Residence

Königssee
- St. Bartholomew's Church

Kulmbach
- Plassenburg Castle

Landshut
- Trausnitz Castle
- Town Residence

Lauenstein near Ludwigsstadt
- Lauenstein Castle

Linderhof
- Linderhof Palace and Park

Munich
- Munich Residence and Court Garden Treasury of the Residence Cuvilliés Theatre

- Feldherrnhalle (Field Marshals' Hall)
- Hall of Fame and Statue of Bavaria
- Nymphenburg Palace and Park, Amalienburg, Badenburg, Pagodenburg, Magdalenenklause Marstallmuseum Nymphenburg Porcelain Museum (Bäuml Collection)
- English Garden

Munich/ Oberschleissheim
- Schleissheim New Palace
- Lustheim Palace

Neuburg/Danube
- Neuburg Palace on the Danube

Neuschwanstein/ Schwangau
- Neuschwanstein Castle

Nuremberg
- Imperial Castle of Nuremberg

Prunn/Altmühltal
- Prunn Castle

Riedenburg
- Rosenburg Castle

Schachen
- King's House on Schachen

Schnaittach
- Rothenburg Fortress

Übersee/Feldwies
- Exter House

Veitshöchheim
- Veitshöchheim Palace and Court Garden

Würzburg
- Würzburg Residence
- Marienberg Fortress

The present first new edition of the Official Guide was written by Werner Helmberger on the basis of the previous editions by Heinrich Kreisel, Erich Bachmann and Burkard von Roda. The sections by Bachmann on the Court Garden, Jost Albert on the kitchen garden and von Roda on the Ingelheim Rooms have been taken over largely unchanged. The section on the State Gallery was contributed by Andreas Schumacher and the short description of the University of Würzburg's Martin von Wagner Museum by Jochen Griesbach and Damian Dombrowski.

Picture credits:
Bayerische Staatsgemäldesammlung: pp. 128, 134, 137, 138
Bayerisches Staatsministerium der Finanzen, für Landesentwicklung und Heimat: Inside front cover
Brandl, Anton J.: Front cover, pp. 3, 4, 7, 8, 20, 37, 42, 44, 48–49, 69
Bunz, Achim: pp. 12, 13, 24–25, 60–61, 64–65, 66–67, 71, 72, 74–75, 77, 78
Gaasch, Uwe: pp. 23, 162, 165, 169
Kunstverlag E. V. König: p. 107
Martin von Wagner Museum: pp. 172, 175, 177, 179, 180, 181, 182, 187
Schneider, Toni: pp. 54, 115
All others: Bayerische Schlösserverwaltung: Tanja Mayr/Rainer Herrmann/ Maria Scherf etc.

Plan of the Court Garden: Norbert Nordmann;
Kochan & Partner Munich
Maps of the main palace: Wilhelm Schott

1st edition of the new version
© Bayerische Verwaltung der staatlichen Schlösser, Gärten und Seen, Munich 2018
Project manager: Kathrin Jung
Edited by Claudia Forchel
Editorial assistance: Anne-Sophie Schultes
Translated by Sue Bollans
Graphic design: Barbara Markwitz, Munich
Lithography: Reproline Genceller, Munich
Printed by: Aumüller Druck, Regensburg
ISBN 978-3-941637-51-1
Printed in Germany